Tunnel to Eternity

Tunnel to Eternity

Beyond Near-Death

Leon Rhodes

with a foreword by
Kenneth Ring

CHRYSALIS BOOKS
West Chester, Pennsylvania

Portions of this book were originally self-published by the author as *Tunnel to Eternity: Swedenborgians Look at the Near-Death Experience* (Bryn Athyn, Pennsylvania, 1996).

Library of Congress Cataloging-in-Publication Data

Rhodes, Leon S.
    Tunnel to eternity : beyond near-death / Leon Rhodes : with a foreword by Kenneth Ring.
        p.   cm.
    Originally published: Bryn Athyn, PA. : L.S. Rhodes, 1996.
    Includes bibliographical references
    ISBN 0-87785-378-9
        1. Future life—New Jerusalem Church.   2. Near-death experiences—Religious aspects—New Jerusalem Church.   3. New Jerusalem Church—Doctrines.   4. Swedenborg, Emanuel, 1688–1772.   I. Title.
BX8729.F8R46   1997
236'.1'088284—DC21
                                                                97–24863
                                                                    CIP

Edited by Susan Flagg Poole
Designed by Vivian Bradbury
Cover design by Vivian Bradbury.
Cover art: Detail of *Ascent into the Heavenly Paradise,* by Hieronymus Bosch c. 1521. Original in Palazzo Ducale, Venice, Italy. Transparency provided by Scala/Art Resource, NY.

Typeset in Caslon 224 Book by Sans Serif, Inc., Saline, MI
Printed in the United States of America

Chrysalis Books is an imprint of the Swedenborg Foundation, Inc. For more information, contact:
    Chrysalis Books
    Swedenborg Foundation
    320 North Church Street
    West Chester, PA 19380

Dedicated to hundreds of friends who
died and later told me about it

Everything that is sensitive and alive is spirit, and everything in us from head to toe is alive and sensitive. That is why, when a body is separated from the spirit, which is called dying, we are still ourselves, and still alive.

Emanuel Swedenborg, *Heaven and Hell* 443

Contents

Foreword

by Kenneth Ring, Ph.D.

No one has done more to demonstrate the relevance of the teachings of Emanuel Swedenborg to the understanding of the near-death experience (NDE) than the author of this book, Leon Rhodes. It was he who, in the immediate aftermath of the publication of Raymond Moody's ground-breaking work, *Life After Life*, in 1975, saw the connection and seized the opportunity to expatiate upon it. What Dr. Moody had briefly alluded to in his book—and even then only as an afterthought—was that the later writings of the great Swedish scientist and seer, set down more than two hundred years before the advent of modern NDE research, had already provided a clear description of all the essential features and insights of the NDE itself.

But Leon did more than point out and elaborate upon these undeniable and uncanny prefigurative parallels. It was his chief contribution to the field of near-death studies, in the early days of that then-fledgling enterprise, to insist that the value of studying Swedenborg's writings went far beyond what Moody had emphasized, which was merely the congruence between Swedenborg's experienced-based dicta concerning the entrance into the life beyond death and contemporary NDE accounts. Leon, in an article expressly commissioned for one of the first issues of *The Journal of Near-Death Studies*, ably made clear that, whereas the typical NDEr is blessed with a fleeting glimpse of the afterdeath realms, lasting in most cases not more than a moment or two, Swedenborg—because he could journey there at will and did so repeatedly during the last twenty-seven *years* (!) of his life—could and did provide a comprehensive picture of the world the NDE only foreshadows.

A modest man himself, Leon did not mention another quality of Swedenborg's that gives added value to his testimony concerning these realms. But as someone who has no personal affiliation with Swedenborgianism as such but only a deep admiration for the profundity and value of Swedenborg's writings on the nature of the spiritual world, I can more easily assert what Leon's reticence prevented: Swedenborg was not only a person of the most extraordinary intellectual gifts whose creative work in a variety of scientific fields still astonishes us today; he was also certifiably one of the spiritual giants of all time. What modern near-death experiencer could claim such credentials or even remotely rival Swedenborg's authority and monumental contributions to our understanding of the spiritual world? Thus, both Swedenborg's remarkable intelligence *and* his extensive sojourns into the world beyond death make his writings of paramount importance for anyone who would seek to inquire into the full implications of the life beyond death of which the NDE is only the (literally) heart-stopping prelude. And more than this, Swedenborg's writings tell us not simply about the life to come but how to live while in this temporary physical vehicle so that we can begin to fashion ourselves with spiritual discernment into the person we wish to be when we come into the light of what William Blake called "Eternity's sunrise."

In this book, the culmination of his career as the leading interpreter of Swedenborg's vision in relation to the NDE, Leon Rhodes adumbrates the essence of the glory that awaits us, according to Swedenborg, when we make the transition from the vicissitudes of earthly life to the blessedness of true life. Yet *Tunnel to Eternity* makes no pretense to be more than an introduction to the grand sweep of Swedenborg's encompassing writings. Its spirit is deliberately invitational rather than didactically expository because it is Leon's intention to lead the interested reader gradually from the mere suggestiveness of NDEs into the richness of Swedenborg's world. Therefore, this book, as full of insight and Leon's wisdom and characteristic humor as it is, is mainly meant to serve as a spur to the reader to explore the treasury of spiritual revelations to be found in Swedenborg's own extensive publications. As a bridge between the phenomenon of the NDE and the peerless Swedenborgian vision, Leon has performed his task admirably and with great skill. Thus, with the publication of this book, we now have the definitive expression of Leon Rhodes' distinctive and invaluable work to enlarge our understanding of the NDE. For this achievement, Leon deserves our deepest thanks and praise indeed.

Acknowledgments

This book is the product of more than twenty years of interest in the phenomenon now known as the near-death experience, or NDE.

Even a small book does not just happen. First, I would like to thank Dr. Kenneth Ring, a leading scholar in the near-death experience, whose encouragement and friendship I treasure. Ken and his associates at the International Association for Near-Death Studies (IANDS) have earned my respect for their work in gaining serious recognition of the near-death experience phenomenon, and I am indebted to Ken for writing the foreword.

Next, beginning with Dr. Raymond Moody, I want to thank the many authors, scholars and "experiencers" from all over the world who took this strange phenomenon and converted it into a respectable and intellectually challenging part of our lives—and our deaths.

This book could not have been completed without my beloved wife Judy, whose gentle but effective needling enabled me to finish the job. She was understanding about my reasons for letting the manuscript sit forlornly in my computer for weeks at a time, but deftly maneuvered me back to writing at just the right moment. It was then that my charming niece, Michelle Rose, skillfully keyed in parts of the manuscript and put it together. I add my thanks to the Rev. Donald L. Rose, my mentor throughout it all.

I would also like to thank the Swedenborg Foundation for its interest in preparing this book, which I originally self-published, into a publication for the general reader. In this regard, I owe my gratitude to Susan Flagg Poole, a developmental writer/editor, who revised the manuscript. Finally, my appreciation goes to the Rev. Wendell Barnett who kindly shared parallels he found between the near-death experience and passages from the theological writings of Emanuel Swedenborg.

Introduction

It is an undeniable fact that you (like me) are going to die. We may not have the slightest idea as to when or how, but you will discover as you read this book, death is not really such a frightening passage. We now have powerful evidence from the reports of thousands of experiencers that the inevitable process of dying is not our final chapter.

When you die, as many stories have indicated, you will first become aware of the fact that you are dying and possibly sense some sort of vibration or a rushing sound. You may be conscious of somehow being pulled out of your body. You may find yourself floating up near the ceiling or above your human form, watching what is happening to your lifeless corpse and hearing the comments by the emergency rescue team, hospital staff, family members, or even casual spectators.

It is probable that you will experience a transition that involves traveling through a dark tunnel—drifting slowly or zooming at great speed—and becoming aware that up ahead there is a very bright light. You approach the light. It becomes indescribably brilliant, radiating warmth and love, and seems to have a personality and to be conveying a message of importance.

You may then find yourself in a strange realm of brilliant colors and great beauty, and notice that there are other people around—maybe people you recognize from the past. It is possible you will experience an astonishing life review of everything you have ever done shown in meticulous detail.

Finally, you will encounter some sort of barrier, perhaps a wall or fence, a gate or bridge, or maybe a stream or an invisible border that, if crossed, will take you into a new dimension—a different level of consciousness. There, you may choose to pass that barrier and will begin a great adventure into the unknown. What we do know about this scenario is based on the memories of those who chose to pass that barrier and who almost immediately found that they were back in their discarded bodies. This phenomenon with its many variations was given the name the "near-death experience" (often shortened to NDE) by Raymond Moody in 1975. The one hundred or so cases Moody studied were from those people who elected to return to earthly life with amazing memories of their experiences (and often the urge to write them down).

No two people have the same experience, although there is remarkable consistency in the many thousands that have been described. This has been called "the core experience," which we will be discussing at length. There are other elements in many NDEs, such as smelling a wonderful fragrance or hearing lovely music; but, at times, an experiencer may report something negative or unpleasant. There are also very important aftereffects that take place in an experiencer's life after returning.

There are fascinating parallels between the NDE and the spiritual world described more than two hundred years ago by the Swedish scientist and religious visionary Emanuel Swedenborg. I have read about and listened to many hundreds of NDEs and have been awed by the similarities to what Swedenborg had to say about this transition from life as we know it to life in the next world. His concepts of the world of spirits and the life of heaven and hell apply to this present world, as well as to the afterlife. To illustrate this idea I often refer in the text to books published by Emanuel Swedenborg, who numbered the paragraphs in many of his books and essays. The reference number, therefore, is to a paragraph, not to a page in a specific edition. To avoid footnotes when citing other material, references to most sources have been kept within the narrative and can be used for further reading.

As the interest in the near-death experience has grown, a number of organizations around the world hold monthly meetings, publish newsletters, and collect information to increase the already voluminous literature of this subject. Most of these organizations would welcome new members and the sharing of new adventures into this land of the world beyond. My sources for many of the experiences described in this book are from letters from around the world and personal accounts given at NDE meetings.

If you, the reader, have had such an experience, or if you know of someone who has returned from the threshold of death with an exciting adventure to describe, you might find there is an NDE organization somewhere in your area. Start by writing out your own near-death experience; give pertinent information about the experience, such as the describing the circumstances bringing it about; then share it. You will find that you are not alone in having had such an adventure. There is still a great deal to be learned about the NDE; and a new book, lecture, article, or informal report may enrich our knowledge of this fascinating phenomenon. After all, in a very real way, you might be providing information about a place we will all enter one of these days.

Leon S. Rhodes
Bryn Athyn, Pennsylvania

Tunnel to Eternity

§ 1 §

Discovering the
Near-Death Experience

In 1975, Mockingbird Books, in preparation for publishing a new title, contacted its author, a medical student named Raymond Moody. The publisher felt the manuscript was a little skimpy and needed to be fleshed out with additional material. Moody's wife, Louise, suggested that the couple visit the public library in Atlanta to see what else they could find on the subject of dying.

They found material to expand and amplify Moody's study of what happens to people when they come to the end of this life. In one chapter, Moody cited a few cryptic references in the Old Testament and selections from the writings of the Apostle Paul in the New Testament. He also referred to the works of the Greek philosopher Plato. In *The Republic*, Plato describes a soldier named Er who had visions of an afterlife, then returned into his body, which was lying on his funeral pyre. Moody also found fascinating material in the *Tibetan Book of the Dead*, but then he came upon a book called *A Compendium of the Theological and Spiritual Writings of Emanuel Swedenborg,* first published in 1853. This book contains selections from the voluminous spiritual writings of Swedenborg. Descriptions about the process of dying and the life after death are scattered throughout thirty or more volumes of inspired writing.

Swedenborg's name is not widely known, but his works are held in high esteem by many people around the world, with numerous centers, including the small community of Bryn Athyn, a few miles north of Philadelphia, my birthplace and hometown. A woman I knew who freely distributed Swedenborg's books to libraries and bookstores for many years called me one day in 1975.

"Leon, there is a new book just published that has nearly six pages from Swedenborg!" She knew that this would interest me greatly. I not only quickly obtained and read a copy of Moody's *Life After Life*, but promptly wrote to him in Georgia.

Raymond Moody contacted me and admitted that he was quite surprised to find a community like Bryn Athyn, populated almost exclusively by people who accept Swedenborg's remarkable theological writings as inspired. This small community has found a greater understanding of this life by studying what Swedenborg had to say about the next. And many have found that Swedenborg's writings have opened their eyes to a broader experience of the spiritual world because Swedenborg spoke with angels while he was still alive. For instance, in his first theological work, *Arcana Coelestia* 5,[1] Swedenborg says,

> It has been granted me now for some years to be constantly and uninterruptedly in company with spirits and angels, hearing them speak and in turn speaking with

---

[1]As is customary in Swedenborg studies, the number following a title refers to a paragraph or section number, which is uniform in all editions, rather than to a page number.

them. In this way it has been given me to hear and see wonderful things in the other life which have never before come to the knowledge of any man[:] . . . the state of souls after death; hell, or the lamentable state of the unfaithful; heaven, or the blessed state of the faithful; and especially in regard to the doctrine of faith which is acknowledged in the universal heaven.

This is an astonishing claim. It is an important beginning to our consideration of the unavoidable transition from this earthly life to a higher and more important realm of consciousness. It is this transition that now carries the label "near-death experience."

My next exposure to the near-death experience resulted from reading a small item in a Philadelphia newspaper announcing a meeting on the subject of the NDE. The Spiritual Frontiers Fellowship sponsored the meeting, which featured the psychologist Kenneth Ring. I attended that meeting, but sat in the back of the audience.

At the end of his explanation of the NDE, Dr. Ring asked if anyone in the audience had questions or comments, asking the speakers to give their names and explain their interest. I stood to identify myself.

"I'm Leon Rhodes, and I am a Swedenborgian."

Ring immediately responded, "Oh, if you're a Swedenborgian, come up here, because you know more about this than I do!"

Those words—"Come up here"— profoundly affected me, and ultimately led me to the writing of this book (which I originally titled "Come Up Here"). Ring's affirmation of my own beliefs meant a great deal to me.

Over the next few years, interest in the NDE dramatically increased, and the International Association for

Near-Death Studies (IANDS) was organized. Because of my background as a professional copywriter, I volunteered to help with the IANDS newsletter, *Vital Signs*, and later became a vice president of the organization. IANDS was not the only organization, however, eager to explore this amazing topic. George Gallup, Jr., the famous pollster, conducted a study to find out how common the near-death experience might be. The findings, published in *Adventures in Immortality* (1982), were astonishing. Using standard polling techniques, Gallup determined that *eight million people in the United States had NDEs*. Shortly after that, a subsequent poll expanded this number to thirteen million, an impressive population.

Ideas of the Afterlife

Emanuel Swedenborg, honored scientist and philosopher, writes throughout the thirty volumes of his theological works that what we think of as the process of dying is actually a transition. It is a transition from a "preparation," which we call life and which might last from a few moments to a ripe old age, into the "real life" for which we were created. He describes the transition in this way:

> When the body is no longer able to perform the bodily functions in the natural world . . ., man is said to die. This takes place when the respiration of the lungs and the beatings of the heart cease. But the man does not die; he is merely separated from the bodily part that was of use to him in the world. . . . It is said that the man himself continues to live since man is not a man because of his body but because of his spirit, for it is the spirit that thinks in

man. . . . Evidently, then, the death of man is merely his passing from one world into another.

Heaven and Hell 445

The near-death experience, then, is not the afterlife. As Kenneth Ring once remarked to me, "Near-death experiencers have had a glimpse through the doorway into the afterlife; Swedenborg explored the whole house!" The near-death phenomenon, as you will see, is a fascinating and broad subject and quite important since it involves eternity, which is a very long time indeed.

To begin with, people's ideas of the afterlife have been closely associated with religious ideas. We all have one paramount question: "Will I be rewarded for a good life, or punished for my bad behavior?" This leads to the dominant question of whether there will be a last judgment in which all our misdeeds and errors will be weighed against our attempts to behave as we should. Many of the rituals that developed around the treatment of the bodies of the newly deceased have less to do with restoring the dead to life than with helping the departed spirit to survive in an afterlife existence. Embalming, wrapping, burying, and making either sarcophagi or funeral statues preserve the memory of the deceased individual. Nearly every graveyard is a veritable archive for historians.

Our ancestors gave a lot of thought as to what should be done after a particular person stopped breathing. There are elaborate tombs and monuments everywhere, but many people today are content with unadorned coffins, headstones, and graves inscribed with "Here Lies . . ." or "R.I.P." For most people, holding a simple ceremony with a burial or cremation is sufficient. Final rites in modern culture have become primarily a procedure for putting a friend to rest in dignity—but no more.

The powerful idea that a person "is not dead, but sleeping" developed over time. If we examine this persistent idea, it is clear that a dead person is entitled to be handled with respect, but also that there is something more to come in the future. This is an idea of great importance and may involve religious beliefs about the Last Judgment, or may take the form of widely held beliefs in reincarnation, where the departed will return as a different person (or perhaps a lower form of animal).

Since it is not entirely clear when the Last Judgment will happen (though many have made predictions), or when "the last trumpet" will sound, it is not surprising that people have wondered just what the dead loved one is going to be doing in the meantime. There are persistent beliefs in ghosts, leprechauns, ghouls, and a vast array of manifestations of departed souls, even fairies, devils, and angels. A surprising number of people even believe that the spirits of decomposing bodies in our cemeteries can somehow wander abroad.

An idea that becomes as widely spread and as persistently held as the belief that supernatural beings lurk in just about every shadow should be taken seriously. These beliefs may not necessarily be true, but they are products of some inborn belief that keeps our ancestors *alive*. This inborn belief preserves the idea that the death of the physical body is not the end of a human life. In other words, our ancestors took spirits and "things that go bump in the night" seriously because the idea preserved the essential belief that, although the body dies, there is something beyond the funeral; the grave is *not* the end. There is, in fact, a spirit world.

The best way to understand the afterlife is to learn about it from an experiencer who has been there, who has arrived at the port of entry and had a brief look-around. Emanuel Swedenborg wrote that he spent twenty-seven years moving freely back and forth between this material world and the spiritual world beyond. It will help, in considering this fascinating claim, to know more about him.

Emanuel Swedenborg

The son of a distinguished Lutheran bishop, Emanuel Swedenborg was born in 1688 as the Age of Enlightenment was dawning. His childhood included excellent schooling, an association with thoughtful people, and a notable interest in abstract matters. He had an inquiring mind and an intense interest in philosophical questions. Most of his childhood was spent in the Swedish university town of Uppsala, where his father was a professor of theology, and where Swedenborg was educated. He studied just about all of the sciences of his day, made many significant scientific discoveries, and published books and essays on a great variety of subjects, including chemistry, hydraulics, crystallography, biology, and anatomy. Swedenborg spoke and wrote several languages, including Latin. He was credited with the invention of mining equipment, a flying machine (the first with correct aerodynamic features), a hot-air stove, a mechanical carriage, a submarine, and a universal musical instrument. Honored as a statesman (a member of the Swedish Parliament) and widely known as a philosopher, psychologist, engineer, and craftsman, Swedenborg was respected and recognized by the scientists of his day and by the Swedish royal family.

Then, in the 1740s, Swedenborg began to have dreams and waking visions that he recorded in an extensive diary.

He came to recognize them as calling him to a new mission. Swedenborg claimed that his "spiritual eyes were opened" so that he could see into the spiritual world. He became aware that, with his "intromission into heaven and hell," he could reveal the wonders of the life after death in God's kingdom.

His scientific writing and publishing ceased; and after a hiatus, a remarkable new work was published in Latin, *Arcana Coelestia* (Heavenly Secrets). This amazing work is currently published in twelve volumes and contains a detailed explanation of an "internal sense" or inner meaning of the books of Genesis and Exodus. Within the stories of creation, the Garden of Eden, the Flood, the lives of the Hebrew patriarchs, and the escape from slavery in Egypt, there is a divine allegory with profound meanings not previously known. A series of short essays with titles such as "The Light in Which Angels are Living," "The Paradise Gardens of Angels and their Dwelling Places," and "The Speech of Angels and Spirits" appear between the chapters of the *Arcana*.

In 1758 Swedenborg published another remarkable book, *Heaven and Hell*, which addressed many of the topics concerning angels and spirits, and provided a veritable guidebook to the realms beyond our universe. This was, and continues to be, Swedenborg's most popular work. It provides a concise, yet detailed, description of the spiritual world, including angels and other spirits, both good and bad.

Swedenborg published dozens of theological books and gave most of them away. His writings are very powerful, but he did not attempt to organize a new religion based on his spiritual experiences. It was not until about fifteen years after his death in 1772 that the first group of his readers gathered to establish a religious organization.

Experiences of Dying

Looking beyond what we can see and hear, we may discover that dying is not as bad as we might think. First of all, we may wish for an end to the suffering that often precedes the actual event of dying. Many of the various life-threatening conditions we encounter will often be uncomfortable at best. This is perhaps the main reason that we associate dying with suffering, and it may be the reason we fear death. But the evidence from the near-death experience is surprising and comforting.

Under most imaginable circumstances, the dying moments of a person as he or she encounters an NDE are far different from what we might expect. The millions of experiencers who have reached the point of death are amazingly casual about their first encounter. A great many report that they *are aware* that they are dying. Although they may have endured a long period of genuine suffering, they seem almost to have forgotten this pain altogether. Whether on the operating table or at the site of an automobile collision, the first moments of the NDE are not only pain-free, but are usually reported with phrases such as "a feeling of bliss," "warmth and love," or even "great ecstasy." Even if the out-of-body experience that carries them upwards lets them see their injured bodies, experiencers report that this sight elicits neither shock nor anxiety and is even an indescribably pleasant moment.

There is another astonishing feature of dying that Swedenborg termed "reflection withheld" (*Arcana Coelestia* 2748), a feature he witnessed when he was allowed to view the newly arrived spirits awakening from death in the spirit world. Swedenborg reports that, in this condition, the newly departed appear to be beyond pain—fearless, unconcerned, and quite dispassionate about the situation that ended their physical existence.

Is it not surprising that so many near-death experiencers are sure they were floating overhead near the ceiling or hovering above the ambulance? If you suddenly found yourself eight feet in the air, you would probably find it disconcerting, to say the least. But near-death experiencers appear to accept such extraordinary circumstances quite calmly. They are *enjoying* a situation that would normally scare the daylights out of just about anyone.

Certainly, under normal life circumstances, you would be astonished to see your grandfather (who died forty years ago) coming to meet you, looking just fine and much younger than you remember him in his last earthly moments. Such an incident would really be disturbing, unless your reflection was withheld (to think about it differently), precisely what Swedenborg said is the case. When experiencers see long-dead relatives looking fit and young in this beautiful realm, they report being delighted, not at all frightened. The loving God who created us does *not* wish us to suffer—physically or mentally—and is very careful that our transition to the spiritual world will be a pleasant one.

There is overwhelming evidence that, in many situations where a patient has been dying over a fairly long period of time, perhaps in a coma, a remarkable change takes place just before the moment of death. Family members or medical personnel notice a "brightening," a different quality when the fatal condition briefly changes. The patient's eyes may open, and sometimes there is verbal expression of a vision, just a few moments before the long-awaited release occurs. In the American Bible Belt, this change is commonly called "angel gazing." Indeed, in a small work entitled *Five Memorable Relations*, Swedenborg wrote that when newcomers first awaken in the spiritual world, angels come to them for the sake of wishing them a favorable arrival; the newcomers are greatly delighted with these conversations because, at first, they think that they are living still in the former world.

Although there is a general consistency in the reports of experiencers and an orderliness about NDEs, in spite of differences in details, sequence, depth, and duration of the adventure, not all returning people describe their experiences as the same.

There are many elements of the NDE, and not everyone has a profound experience. Some people return early in the experience because a doctor, nurse, or friend resuscitated them before they had a chance to undergo a life review, which comes in the later stages of the core experience. Through the years I have received many letters from people describing their near-death experiences, and have found that the effect of the experience may vary depending on the length of the NDE. A woman in Australia wrote to me of her experience while undergoing a major operation:

> I found myself flying over the city and suburbs until I paused over my parents' back garden. My mother emerged to hang out some washing. A crow was perched on the clothesline and when my mother saw it she looked worried. [Her mother later confirmed this.] Then I became aware of a tremendous suction behind me, and turning around, found myself being drawn into a huge, swirling dark tunnel that led slightly upward. Traveling at tremendous speed I saw a speck of light in the far distance, and I felt a great desire to reach that light. It grew larger until it was a glorious golden disc and the sides of the tunnel glistened with a million tiny stars. Then, with a great burst of

light, and rays of light like iridescent arms reaching out to me, I emerged from the tunnel to find a Radiant Being before me. He seemed to be made of love and His voice reached out to me like soothing, golden, liquid music, and I was engulfed in light and love.

In another situation, a woman who suffered from asthma as a child remembered the experience she had when she was only three years old. She described what happened when she was struggling to breathe:

. . . and then I didn't breathe anymore and I found myself at the top of the room near the ceiling, looking down at this body on the bed. I noticed it was small. Then all of a sudden I was in this tunnel, very dark except for these rectangular mirrors of different colors. I started up the tunnel, slow at first, then speeding up, like the speed of light. The little mirrors were pulled with my increasing speed and pretty soon formed a focused light and all of a sudden I was in total white, standing on the steps of a cathedral that was like crystal. You could put your hand through the building, and it pulsed and shimmered.

In a third experience, a young man skating on the local reservoir fell through the ice; and as he approached hypothermia, he could scarcely move. He recounts the experience:

In silence I went down, my arms floating above my head like a rag doll. Then I was no longer afraid and a warm feeling came over me. I felt very peaceful and physically very comfortable. It felt like I was being drawn backwards down a long, dark tube, sucked past a wall of spongy black cotton. Over my shoulder I saw what looked like the sun, it had a soft yellow glow like a buttery biscuit.

There are noticeable similarities among these stories, yet each is unique. They do not seem to be the sort of thing a person could easily make up. These are just little nuggets from experiences that have much more to them. Entire books are written on single experiences, such as Dannion Brinkley's *Saved by the Light* and Betty J. Eadie's *Embraced by the Light*. There are thousands more like these accounts that I have listened to or read about.

There are so many different aspects and new things to learn from each death scenario because NDEs can vary as to the sequence and the elements. It is important to keep in mind, however, that the NDE is not like dreams or hallucinations, mainly in that there is a "sequence" and familiar pattern to NDEs. Although I do not know of any meticulous study of how long a near-death experience lasts, it is usually described as lasting for only a short period in our time—generally a period when there is apparently no breath or heartbeat—or it could last as long as twenty minutes. A powerful account of an NDE that lasted more than twenty minutes is described by Dannion Brinkley in his work *Saved by the Light*, perhaps the longest on record in which time could be measured. Before publication of Raymond Moody's historic *Life after Life*, Brinkley had been struck by lightning and "killed." (Moody later called Brinkley's NDE "one of the most remarkable.") Brinkley experienced a tunnel, a being of light "like a bag full of diamonds," and a fantastic life review. But most notably, he recovered twenty-eight minutes later with astonishing psychic powers.

As we know, many NDEs have been described in such a way that they fill large books, and the numerous television programs or reenactments of them appear to involve only a short period of time. That "other world," however, is one without time or space, and experiencing this timeless state profoundly affects those who have been there and have returned. They had brief glimpses into an existence of more complete knowledge.

While no two NDEs are precisely alike, there is a striking consistency and enough general agreement to provide some proof of the validity of the NDE. When we think of paranormal experiences, we soon realize that there is an infinite variety. In the early days of NDE research, it was striking how many people under different circumstances told of an out-of-body experience, a tunnel, a bright light with a personality, a beautiful realm with recognizable people, and a wide-screen, "3-D" life review. The recurrence of those elements alone would have provided some assurance that these were not hallucinations, not the result of endorphins, oxygen deprivation, medications, or trauma. Skeptical people, especially well-qualified medical personnel, offered many explanations of the NDEs. But it was not long before some of those arguments were abandoned, simply because the experiences themselves seemed to have logic, order, and meaning.

Awareness of Dying

The variety of experiencers and the similarities of their stories involve a great deal more than the mere symptoms of trauma. The many thousands of published NDEs are far more consistent than would have been possible if these were concoctions or fantasies.

Circumstances are far too varied to suggest that the NDE

is a natural result of the injury, illness, or shock. Anyone who has been following NDE literature is well aware that a recognizable NDE can come about following a drowning, childbirth, an auto accident, electrocution, asphyxiation, improper medication, suicide, or heart attack. My own correspondence files bulge with letters from a man named Mickey who had his NDE while an attempt was being made on his life.

Mickey was born into a dysfunctional family of professional thieves. He was raised to be a thief and got very good at it; however, he stole a car from another gang member one day and was seriously injured while doing it. He had a complete near-death experience. Before his NDE, Mickey states, he did not have a conscience; but after, he never wanted to steal again. He is in prison for his pre-NDE crimes, but he has become a valuable person working to improve prison conditions. He is even grateful for the fact that he has lots of free time to study legal books, as well as those of Swedenborg.

The NDE properly speaking usually follows "the cessation of life signs." In other words, the individual is at the brink of death. The person stops breathing, has no detectable pulse, and even shows no brain waves on a monitor. For all practical purposes, this person has reached the point of death. Yet somehow he or she, though unconscious, is far from being unaware. An observer may consider the afflicted person to be either unconscious or dead. Yet, upon recovery, the victim will report an awareness of what was happening, such as the efforts to revive him or her and the panic or shock of onlookers. Thus, consciousness here means a higher level of consciousness, since all the observable symptoms attest to the experiencer's being without sensation.

I again must inject a caveat. Not all people have an NDE

simply because they have reached the condition of "clinical death." There are countless cases in which the patient reaches the threshold of death, recovers, and cannot recall any of the core experience elements of an NDE. I know of a woman who had no recollection of such an experience, yet she readily acknowledged that the few moments during which she had been "dead" had profoundly affected her. She now had no fear of death and felt keenly that she knew what life after death would be like.

Moreover, the NDE phenomenon should not be considered a peculiarity that affects only those whose hearts and lungs stop functioning. It affects many people in a variety of circumstances. This fact opens up the reality of another existence.

The spiritual realm that experiencers briefly visit is the *real* world, the world that is ever-present. Swedenborg reports from his own experience that the spiritual world is all around us, though we are not conscious of it unless there is reason to be. Our senses tell us that *this* material world is the real world because we can see, hear, feel, taste, and smell some aspect of it. But the unseen, unheard, unfelt spiritual world is not only around us now, it is the world for which we were created.

Indeed, there is a wide spectrum of spiritual experiences that are not near-death experiences but that testify to the existence of a concurrent spirit world. The history of humanity is filled with an amazing array of instances in which this crude physical realm around us somehow dissolves, permitting a glimpse into the genuine spiritual world. Humans have visions of many kinds without approaching a condition of clinical death, for example and most notably, religious visions, such as those of St. John of the Cross or Teresa of Avila. Even our dreams or imaginings, like our hallucina-

tions or deliriums, involve a change in the level of consciousness. Whether we are inclined to consider those visions and dreams to be real, they can profoundly affect us
and how we live.

One explanation of visions is offered by Swedenborg,
who has much to say about the influence of the good and
bad spirits around us. These spirits play major roles in our
moods, fears, emotions, and secret passions. This subject is
of considerable importance when our lives become disori-
ented. Swedenborg contends that evil spirits are at work at
times of stress, urging us to choose the wrong path; yet,
these influences are balanced by the efforts of good spirits or
angels. At any rate, the spiritual world around us is a real
thing, with dramatic effects on our lives.

The subject of consciousness itself is an enormous field.
At any given moment, we are surrounded by uncountable
influences, though, fortunately, most of the time we are conscious of only a few things. A few of the sounds causing our
ear drums to flutter have an impact on our consciousness.
Much of our sense of touch is largely dormant at any given
moment; and our wide field of vision includes a myriad of
images that we can ignore until, by conscious effort, we decide to focus on a particular object, such as the spider weav-
ing its web on a nearby window. Even beyond marvelous
sense perceptions, think of the wondrous realm of our imag-
ination, with its own preferences for a favorite color, or
some violent association with an audible or visual symbol.
Consciousness, however, is on a higher level than familiar
sense systems, which might be thought of like cameras or
tape recorders.

Neither can we ignore the effect of what we call "anticipation" in the NDE. This simply involves the extent to
which the expectation of death can be a major factor in the

experience itself. When the possibility of death is occupying the mind, one often becomes conscious of the spiritual world. The person who plans suicide is in a very different frame of mind from that of a teenaged boy who unwisely dives into a pond and unexpectedly strikes his head on a rock. This would apply in a different way to the person who is being readied for major surgery because of a life-threatening problem as compared to the expectations of a woman who is sound asleep when an earthquake brings the walls down on her.

Indeed, the experience of an NDE *before* an injury often happens under stressful conditions. People have jumped off San Francisco's Golden Gate Bridge and had NDEs on their way down to the water because they were expecting to die; but, surprisingly, they landed and lived. In a similar circumstance, skiers have found themselves in situations where they were flying through the air and felt that they would probably not survive the jump. Although they did survive, they had an NDE because of the intense stress from the expectation of death. Another example of an NDE that happened before an injury took place occurred to a man who was trying to escape from a Nazi prison camp. He was running toward a charged wire fence, about to be electrocuted, when he had an NDE before he reached the fence. He was shocked, but did not die.

The anticipation of danger, expectation of death, or fear of painful injury shapes our frame of mind in ways that could well be reflected in the visions that will engulf us. Such factors, I feel strongly, may be important in considering the uncommon but well-known "negative" or "dark" near-death experience, which I discuss later in the book. Carried further, our actual mental condition, as well as our emotional stresses, deserves consideration as we search for the meanings of the near-death experience. It is my firm conviction that something as influential and meaningful as the NDE does not come about just by accident. There have been many NDEs resulting from accidents; but then Swedenborg believed that there is no such a thing as a meaningless accident, as he relates in *Divine Providence* 70 and *Arcana Coelestia* 6493.

Under many circumstances the conditions leading to the point of the NDE involve terror, severe suffering, or frantic efforts to escape the disaster. In other situations, such as during major surgery, an "NDEr" might be under sedation or simply rendered unconscious by a physical injury. Nonetheless, the first awareness of dying is the most striking part of the experience because it is almost invariably described as peaceful, painless, and calm. People try to convey the experience of those first moments using words such as "unconditional love," "ineffable joy," or even "ecstasy"!

This is reassuring. It is also comforting to know that, regardless of appearances to the contrary, when we are at the verge of death, we may find the experience pleasant. People seem to rise above the circumstances of their own deaths. That moment most dreaded by all of us is often described in glowing terms by those who have been there. Imagine how this basic thought can provide a measure of solace as we think of some tragic disaster. We here encounter a phenomenon that involves a certain philosophical outlook.

Divine Mercy at Times of Disaster

Throughout humankind's distressing history of natural disasters, starvation, warfare, torture, or simple physical mishaps, the understandable reaction to the death process has been to question the reason for suffering. "How can a loving and merciful God allow such suffering?" "If God is all powerful and merciful, why do we see so much agony and distress in life?" There may be a tremendous amount of pain involved, even if the moment of death is eased by this incredible sensation of love and elation. But the real anguish associated with death—the death of someone we care about or love—is that, regardless of how pleasant *their* experience is, they are gone, taken from us. This, too, raises the question about how much suffering a loving and merciful God could allow.

Our reaction to the death of a stillborn infant or of a baby lost to Sudden Infant Death Syndrome is hardly comparable to the emotions aroused by the death of hundreds of people in an earthquake or flood, but the child's parents still suffer a life-altering loss. We cannot deal with death as a normal and orderly event when it is the consequence of a terrorist attack or an insane person's wild frenzy. Such deaths seem far removed from the death of an elderly person who has lived a full life, yet who may die of a dreaded illness such as cancer.

The suffering associated with dying distorts the picture, since we can agree that pain and suffering, whether mental or physical, is something to be avoided. Pain and suffering have been built into humanity for a reason. In our own experience, we know that pain protects us. We jerk our hand away from the hot stove before our skin is severely damaged, and even the discomfort from the common cold is a warning to take it easy, get into bed, and perhaps even seek medical help. Without our ability to recognize pain as a warning sign, we would be vulnerable indeed. Whether or not we are willing to carry this thought far enough to see that human suffering is a God-given blessing because we would be in danger without it, we can still recognize the wisdom of the Creator and all the protecting mechanisms that have been instilled in us. The ultimate reason for our suffering might, in the long run, justify our present pain.

Throughout Swedenborg's remarkable theological works, he constantly emphasizes that God's infinite love and mercy are such that all things are directed toward a person's *eternal* happiness. In this life, there are trials and tribulations, pain and suffering, loss and unhappiness; but the essential goal is our eternal end. Though this view may seem simplistic, we can see that this means that, although humans will be subjected to temporal suffering, God's mercy is always guiding us toward enduring happiness.

It is not easy sometimes to accept this argument about a merciful and loving God; but as our beliefs develop and are strengthened, we find that we can look beyond our temporal discomfort with the conviction that it may serve a purpose in the grand scheme. We do not always understand the purpose in our current circumstances since we are always adjusting to the undeniable fact that we live in a world where warfare and injustice are far too common and the innocent are subjected to dreadful cruelties by the evil and heartless. And so, we wonder, "How can a merciful and loving God permit . . . ?"

How can we blame God for cruelties resulting from crime, warfare, and evil conduct? Similar questions arise when we think of floods, earthquakes, volcanic eruptions, drought—any natural disaster. Human suffering, from any number of causes, has long troubled thoughtful people. Swedenborg emphasizes the concept that human suffering itself is never caused by God. One of his most powerful insights is that divine providence guides all events. In Swedenborg's view, everything that happens, regardless of its outward appearance, is under the guidance of providence. This principle of caring foresight operates to keep humanity free. It means that people are free to do good or bad things, and that the laws of nature applying to volcanoes, floods, and droughts are within the laws of order. Divine providence does not *cause* bad things to happen. In the omniscient control of events, God's infinite love and wisdom provides for the eternal welfare of people. God works not for the short-term comfort or welfare of those involved, but for their eternal welfare, since everyone ever born has been created for the greatest happiness that can be achieved without loss of freedom. In order to live in eternal happiness, God allows us to experience distressing, but temporary, unhappiness. As Swedenborg writes in *Arcana Coelestia* 2694, "Those who are being reformed or becoming spiritual are brought into the state of vastation [suffering] or desolation, and when experiencing this state even to the point of despair, they for the first time receive comfort and help from the Lord."

This challenging concept applies to our mental and spiritual suffering just as surely as the physical agonies we associate with death. One of the things often said when a suffering friend has died is "What a blessing!" This is not meant in defiance of the sadness brought on by a loved one's death, but in acknowledgment that the physical pain has ended. Moreover, there can be happiness mixed with the grief when one considers the wonderful journey that is beginning for the deceased. Believing in an afterlife can bring a distinctly different atmosphere to a funeral, memorial service, or other commemoration.

One spring afternoon I drove to our little Swedenborgian community cemetery in Bryn Athyn and felt very much at home. The graveyard, in a wooded area not far from our beautiful cathedral, is naturally unkempt, rather than clipped and mowed. The headstones appear almost random and are seldom elaborate. There are no monuments, though there are small clusters where family graves have been marked, often with a headstone of a husband or wife with the date of death not yet carved. Our interments here, which are reserved for close family and friends, involve a simple ceremony and a prayer, perhaps a hymn. Following the graveside committal, there is a formal worship service for the community, called a "resurrection service," held at the cathedral. People distraught by the death of loved one often leave that service uplifted. The strong belief in a life beyond changes the atmosphere. Rather than saying that a man has recently died, Swedenborgians might say, "He has passed into the spiritual world." Few people here even think of having an open-coffin service, and the local undertakers have become resigned to the fact that most people in our little town have no particular interest in chrome and satin caskets or embalming.

The last time I visited this cemetery, I met a friend whom I had not seen for many years. He had brought his nephew with him, carrying long-handled clippers to cut back the fairly large bushes that had been planted long ago among some family graves. The area is kept rustically attractive by a few volunteers, and an occasional work group has come through after a storm. My friend and I chatted briefly, agreeing that this informality suits both of us perfectly. Placing simple markers for those who leave their bodies to science or choose cremation is enough for us. A great deal of cherished history and pleasant memories can be relived just by strolling among the graves.

Dying—Not as Bad as We Thought

Bad things do happen to good people, whether it be a broken rung on a ladder that results in a fatal fall, or the freak accumulation of a deadly gas in an auditorium that ends the lives of many school children. Tragedies assault the fragile bodies in which we live, bringing us to that point where our heart, lungs, and brain cease to function. We face death and suddenly encounter the conditions that can bring about the near-death experience.

Again, we turn to the point where our bleeding, crumpled body or fractured frame can probably no longer sustain life as we know it, and yet somehow we are conscious of these ghastly circumstances. However, near-death experiencers report that not only were they unaware of enduring great agony, but they were surprisingly dispassionate about the dreadful events that had brought them to this crisis.

It seems fair, then, to contend that a merciful God is guiding us with wondrous tenderness and gentle comfort at this critical moment. Among the overwhelming statistics about near-death experiencers is the fact that virtually all assert, after their experience, that they are not afraid to die. Ponder that fact for a moment. These people have been through a remarkable journey, but are surprisingly relaxed about this circumstance which, for nonexperiencers, is largely terrifying. But this does not mean that the moment is unimportant.

In Swedenborg's theological works, this moment is often the occasion to put ourselves into the caring hands of those lovely beings, our "guardian angels." The subject of angels is a delightful one, and the angels who are given the responsibility of managing our transition from this life to the next are well worth knowing. As Swedenborg describes them, angels are not beautiful winged women with halos, wearing diaphanous gowns and playing harps. They are simply good people who once lived on this earth and died. They are spiritual beings who, by their love and attitude, provide the divine loving care that properly guides us through the critical moment from death to a new life. Their affectionate concern not only brings about a sphere of peace and love, but it shields us from the evil forces eager to take advantage of us during a period of vulnerability.

❧ 2 ❧

The Core Experience

A s I have said, the various stages of near-death that make up the core experience do not strictly conform to a rigid scenario or invariably follow a particular sequence. However, in the primary stage, it is usually true that the experiencer has a surprising consciousness and an awareness of the physical world, regardless that the experiencer can appear unconscious and virtually dead to observers. This phase of the adventure is frequently identified as an out-of-body experience, or OBE, a state that indicates that the experiencer is entering into a higher level of consciousness.

The Out-of-Body Experience

The OBE is an important part of the NDE, usually the beginning phase, in which the person is almost entirely conscious of the physical world. I say "almost" because the experiencer is usually "floating above," hovering near the ceiling of the operating room, looking down on the scene of the accident, or watching the grieving family clustered around the rumpled bed to say their goodbyes.

Often the experiencer describes the beginning of an OBE

with words such as, "I felt myself being drawn up through my head," or "I suddenly found myself floating overhead while the medics were putting my body into the ambulance." These descriptions are of interest because the "myself" is the *true* person, not the injured and dying physical body. This early stage differentiates between the *spirit* of the experiencer and the material flesh that may be no longer capable of sustaining life. The body might just as well rest in peace.

The OBEs associated with reported NDEs come in a remarkable variety, and many of them have interesting features that let us know that we are now in a different realm of consciousness. Yet, in many cases, what the floating spirit observed, and later reported, is astonishingly accurate. The accounts of the experience are often in precise detail, including the conversations heard between attending medical personnel, and following the events as they actually occurred. These accounts are quite significant because they describe events from a particular vantage point. Although the floating personality could see and hear what was going on, the recently vacated body is often in such a situation that it was impossible to see the things described.

For example, Barbara, who has written about her experience, said that her NDE came about while she was undergoing back surgery. She was face down on the operating table with her head buried in a pillow and a towel over her head, yet she accurately reported what the medical team was doing throughout the entire episode.

Sometimes the accounts of the experiencer are unintentionally humorous. One of my favorite examples is also from a hospital setting. A woman, who was dying, was able to watch and hear two medical attendants. She heard one of them say that he hoped the patient wouldn't take up too much of their time dying because he had a date later that evening and needed to get going. Such reports are important because they attest to a situation that can be verified. In contrast to those things *seen* by the experiencer in the after-life, these reports are about the physical setting of the death scene and other people involved, that is, what we the living might consider the "real" scene.

In another account by a floating experiencer, a woman describes the medical charts at the head of other beds in the room. The truly remarkable feature of this NDE account was that the experiencer was blind. Indeed, Kenneth Ring, probably the foremost spokesman for the NDE, conducted an extensive study of NDEs experienced by blind people, including those who had been born blind. Many blind people could see things that they had never seen before during their NDEs. It may be that the those who are physically blind can see during such an episode because, as Swedenborg said, "sight is not in the eye." The eye is the organ, but it is the *mind* that sees:

> Unless it were the spirit within the body that saw the things taken in by the eye as the organ of sight, the spirit would be unable to see anything in the next life, when, in fact, it is destined to behold countless and astonishing sights which the eye of the body cannot possibly see.
>
> *Arcana Coelestia* 2588

The OBE, however, is not exclusively reserved for people on the threshold of death. Swedenborg, who was not near death, described his OBE in *Heaven and Hell* 449: "I was permitted to see and feel that there was a pulling and drawing forth, as it were, of the interiors of my mind, thus my spirit, from the body." This is a different kind of seeing, but it is consistent with the ability of the mind to observe images that are invisible to the eye. (Is this because the mind is more closely related to the "person" than is the body?) It is noteworthy that the OBE phenomenon is identified by Swedenborg as a characteristic of biblical prophecies and visions. He says that this condition—when the mind is free from the physical body—is called "being in the spirit" and that being "out of the body" is also called "a vision of God" in the spiritual world. Indeed, in his writings, Swedenborg cites no less than sixteen such visions in the Old Testament, including those of Daniel, and finds it to be a main feature of the book of Revelation. If the various NDE study groups want to explore new fields they might take a closer look at the OBE vision. Although the OBE frequently is a part of the NDE, it seems to be a universal and historic experience without the symptoms of a stilled heart, lack of breathing, or serious physical problems.

During the twenty years I have written articles, lectured, and attended meetings on the subject of NDEs, many people have asked if I have ever had a near-death experience. Because of my association with IANDS, I have heard and read about many firsthand NDEs. My own "experience" has been a single out-of-body incident. As with many spiritual experiences, it is not easily put into words.

I was in our living room in front of the fireplace, my elbows on the mantle, looking into the flames of a small fire. I became aware that the mantle, fireplace, and fire slowly dissolved away; and I was able to walk through the fire, coming into a new realm of consciousness. It reminded me of parts of the NDE reported by many experiencers when they find themselves in a new realm, a world of striking beauty with fascinating colors and sights that could be described as "out of this world." Yet, the scene was very real, only unlike anything I had ever seen before. I found myself awed by this setting. Almost immediately as I looked up ahead, I became aware of my father, who had died in February 1964, long before the current interest in near-death experiences began, walking toward me. He came closer; he looked just fine, although I had been at his bedside during his last days as he wasted away and became, somehow, a stranger to my eyes.

Pop enjoyed discussions about life and keeping in touch with me and my young family. As Swedenborgians, we enjoyed casual but fairly serious discussions of Swedenborg's theological writings, especially those relating to the life after death and the spiritual world. We had a pretty good relationship, though probably less overtly affectionate than many paternal friendships, since he was and I am inclined to be reserved and reluctant to display emotion. I loved my father and had great respect for him; and from my school days and early adult life, he had been helpful and very interested in my somewhat unorthodox ventures into the professional theater in New York City. Pop came to see me perform on Broadway in the original production of Thornton Wilder's Pulitzer Prize-winning play *Our Town*. We enjoyed discussing the play's message from the Swedenborgian point of view, since Wilder had been a reader of Swedenborg. In the play, the young heroine, Emily, having died in childbirth, is allowed to go back and revisit her home, reliving her twelfth birthday. Now, I was in a situation where Pop was revisiting me.

During my out-of-body experience, Pop came forward and we met comfortably. He assured me, although without speaking, that those talks we'd had about affirming the reality of the spiritual world were quite true. In retrospect, I wonder that I was not astonished or even incredulous of our meeting; I knew instinctively that this was not intended to be a discussion so much as the delivery of a simple message. There was no need for a response, and I again became aware of the fire and the mantlepiece. Our visit was over. It was a simple, yet eloquent, out-of-body experience.

The Spiritual World

My experience, and the OBE in general, is a dramatic introduction to the spiritual world. Swedenborg stresses that the *real* world is the spiritual world of which we are rarely conscious. Not only is there this marvelous, unseen, unheard universe around us at all times, with spirits greatly influencing our ideas and our emotions, but there is a feeling of their presence that we can come to recognize. We can and do actually "choose" to associate ourselves with these unseen spirits and their effects on our lives. Our association with good spirits can greatly enrich our ideas and our emotions, whereas we too often allow or even encourage unruly spirits to arouse moods and thoughts in us detrimental to our spiritual welfare.

An eloquent nineteenth-century Swedenborgian, the Rev. Chauncey Giles, wrote a superb study that presents a rational view on the subject of death. *The Nature of Spirit and of Man as a Spiritual Being* was first published in 1867 and later translated into several languages. Giles writes that the spiritual world

is here, is everywhere around us, and is separated from us only by the thin veil of matter. We are in it now, though unconscious of it. Man is a spirit in the human form, and when the veil of matter is withdrawn, the spiritual world in which he was already living is revealed to him. He has not gone to any remote place. He is not changed. He sees the beings who were around him, and just as near him, before the veil was withdrawn from his eyes.

Man is essentially a spiritual being, a spirit in the human form, with a complete human organization, having spiritual senses adapted to spiritual objects, as his natural senses are adapted to natural objects; that the material body is no part of the man [and you may be sure that "man" in its true sense means both male and female] . . . but is simply the sustaining basis and containant of those spiritual substances of which the man himself is formed, the instrument he uses to perfect his complete spiritual organization, and lay the foundation for the superstructure of his future life.

The spiritual world, though unseen, is all around us during our lifetime. Our place and circumstance in that realm are the reasons for our human birth and for our being prepared to live as an eternal beings.

We have seen that the OBE is part of the near-death experience in which the dying spirit leaves the body, but is still very much in this world. The experiencer is conscious of the surroundings, aware of the actions and words of other people, and able to observe the circumstances that may very well be the last moments of his or her earthly life. The NDEr floating overhead has a surprisingly dispassionate attitude as to what has happened and does not share the grief of the sobbing friends and relatives. The experiencer is a reliable reporter in spite of the fact that the nearly lifeless body is his or her own. The NDEr's point of view is totally different from those of other participants or spectators because it is based on an experience that is truly out of this world.

The Dark Tunnel

An OBE, however, is only a first, preliminary stage of the core experience. It is common to have an abrupt transition into the second stage, the now familiar "tunnel" sequence. This awe-inspiring passageway is almost invariably described as very dark. There is actually a fascinating portrayal of the near-death experience by Hieronymus Bosch, the famous fourteenth-century painter of allegories, entitled *Ascent into the Heavenly Paradise*, a section of which is featured on the cover of this book. In the picture, there is a "lifeless" body at the bottom of the scene, while extending above the body is a long, dark tunnel. At the far end of the tunnel is a bright light.

The tunnel phase is almost always characterized by darkness, even blackness, followed by or contrasted to a brilliant light. Throughout his works, Swedenborg emphasizes a great variety of symbols. Darkness and light are representative of the obvious ideas of ignorance and knowledge. As he wrote in *Arcana Coelestia* 9642 concerning the imagery in Isaiah 58:10, " 'darkness and thick darkness' denote ignorance of truth and good; while 'light,' and 'the noonday' denote the understanding of them." If we pursue this association, the tunnel phase of the NDE, in all its fascinating variety, can be interpreted as the progression from dark, shadowy ignorance to the astonishing discovery of an altogether new realm.

Moving through the dark tunnel, the NDEr encounters a new meaning to the word "light." Experiencers stress that these are not merely dark tunnels and bright lights. The word *tunnel* is appropriate in some ways, if we imagine going through New York's Holland Tunnel—without any lights—and arriving at Times Square when it is all ablaze. But that isn't the typical near-death experience.

The most frequently heard description of the NDE is that it is "ineffable," that it just cannot easily be described in words. If we think about it, a great many things in our lives cannot be readily described. This is true of even very familiar things like a sunrise, a baby's smile, our favorite piece of music, or a relationship with someone we love. Words are very limited; and in many cases, we do not even attempt to describe something special.

Swedenborg, like most experiencers, says that what awaits us in the spiritual world is indescribable. The things he saw and heard in heaven were incapable of being expressed in words. He said things in heaven were "such as ear hath never heard nor eye seen . . ." For him, spirits had "seen and perceived amazing things, all of which were resplendent . . . with innumerable other things that could not be described in human language even as to a ten-thousandth part" (Heaven and Hell 239, 411). Clearly, when the mind is loosed from the bonds of the physical body, it no longer thinks naturally, but spiritually, and its thoughts are incomprehensible to the natural person.

The tunnel part of the NDE is extraordinary and defies description. An experiencer who attended one of my lectures on the NDE said to me, "Everyone talks about the dark tunnel. The one I saw wasn't just dark; it was so black that it glistened!" Black doesn't mean just the absence of light. Many of the experiencers that I've talked with have struggled to convey what they went through, not just a dark hole, but something "so black I could feel it," or "a fuzzy, warm sort of blackness." One NDEr stated that the tunnel "was so black that I could swim in it!" This is a different level of consciousness, including the sense that the NDEr is progressing *through* the tunnel because there is something waiting. Some say that they "zoom" through darkness at a very high speed, whereas others float gently through. Yet nearly all of them were somehow weightless and traveling effortlessly without support or plan. They were outside of time and space, and not particularly interested in the black void around them. They were more curious about what was waiting for them at the end of the tunnel.

While in this blackness, experiencers are really in a state of questioning. They do not understand their surroundings because none of the familiar laws of physics seems to apply. But there is a *purpose*, a reason that most of them, at that moment, relate to the light up ahead. Often they declare that they are "drawn to the light" and have no consciousness of how to leave the blackness. This must feel like something that we have experienced when we did not know where we were going or what waited for us up ahead.

A Different Kind of Light

In many, if not most, near-death experiences, the tunnel somehow leads to an extraordinary light. In some cases, a tiny light is seen, which grows larger and brighter. This fantastic light seems to be the focal point of the experience and is almost invariably described as bright, "the brightest light ever seen." Swedenborg describes this light as a bright, white light "that becomes a beautiful golden tinge" (*Arcana Coelestia* 185). Even though intense, the light from NDE accounts brings no harm or injury and doesn't hurt the experiencer's eyes. Furthermore, many accounts suggest that this light has a personality, that it exudes qualities of warmth and loving care, and that it conveys an important message. It has even been referred to as a "Being of Light." Indeed, Swedenborg gives a fascinating explanation of how the angels actually experience God in heaven as the sun:

> The Lord is seen as a sun, not in heaven, but high above the heavens; and not directly overhead or in the zenith, but before the faces of the angels at a middle height. He is seen at a considerable distance, in two places, one before the right eye and the other before the left eye. Before the right eye he is seen exactly like the sun, as it were with a glow and size like that of the sun of the world. But before the left eye he is not seen as a sun, but as a moon, glowing white like the moon of our earth, and of like size, but more brilliant, and surrounded with many little moons, as it were, each of them of similar whiteness and splendor.
>
> *Heaven and Hell* 118

Many NDErs identify this loving light as God, Jesus, the Virgin Mary, or an angel. Others describe it as a grandparent or other family member, a "prophet," or simply an indescribably wise person. This light has a special message for the experiencers, or it has something to tell them that gives meaning to the entire near-death experience. For a significant number of experiencers, the message was simple: "It's not your time." The experiencer has to go back and return to a physical existence.

There is something strange about those who were told that it was not their time. They perhaps wanted to explore this higher realm of consciousness further, yet were simply not allowed to make this transition. They might have come to the end of their NDE and awakened with little or no memory, giving an incomplete picture of their wonderful adventure. Modern resuscitation techniques are almost an invasion of the NDE. Some experiencers disliked coming back, wishing they had died. Lee Woofenden, in his graduate thesis at the Swedenborg School of Religion (1995), states the following:

> Coming back to earth after visiting the spiritual world can be difficult. Once we have experienced the beauty, joy, light, and love of that world, this world can seem dark and painful. Yet most NDEers come back with a new sense of the spiritual depth within, and a sense that they have work to do here. Experiencing the spiritual world does not automatically transform us into angels. It only gives us a glimpse of the path. That path lies through learning to understand and love each other.

The indescribably brilliant light often sensed as an all-loving, all-knowing person is the key element of the NDE. This is especially true when the NDEr has the overwhelming feeling of being in the presence of God. This is not something to be taken lightly. It is a profound idea that, when we leave this life and enter God's kingdom, we will face God in many ways.

In Genesis, we read that no one can look on the face of God and live. In the New Testament, we learn that no one has seen God at any time. Swedenborg affirms the belief that humans cannot actually see the infinite God. God's infinite majesty would consume us as though we had ventured into the sun itself. Yet, Swedenborg also writes that we will encounter a heavenly being as we come to the threshold of the spiritual world. The idea is that, although the face, the "brilliance of God," could not be endured by humans, we will be greeted by a heavenly being and that this heavenly being will be recognized by us as the spirit who has all the qualities needed to greet us and welcome us.

It is not surprising, then, that for many experiencers, especially younger ones, the dazzling welcoming spirit may be identified in their minds as Jesus Christ or as a central figure from their religious upbringing. What is your idea of God? What *is* the infinite God, the all-loving Creator, the maker of heaven and earth, and the essence of all true love and wisdom? A fundamental Swedenborgian concept is that God is the "divine-human." God is the unimaginable force with those human qualities with which we all are endowed. We are human because God is human. It was necessary for God to take on humanity so that we could actually *see* those human qualities. For the inhabitants of Israel two thousand years ago, Jesus came as a noble teacher who worked great miracles. For Christians through the ages, Jesus is the Christ, the incarnate God, the Son of God, whose life and works are described in the New Testament.

In *Heaven and Hell* 450, Swedenborg explains that there are special spirits (or angels) who have unique qualities that make them suitable as welcomers for newcomers:

> Angels from the Lord's spiritual kingdom appear to roll off, as it were, a coat from the left eye toward the bridge of the nose. . . . There is a slight sense of light, but very dim, inducing spiritual thought. The angels are extremely careful that only such ideas as savor of love shall proceed from the one resuscitated.

These angels will appear to us in a nonthreatening form, indeed in a form that is full of love. Depending on our frame of mind, we might see these angels with or without wings. A Christian might identify such an angel as Jesus Christ and sense an all-powerful love and infinite wisdom. A Jewish child might see Moses. An Arab child might see Mohammed. The message that these spirits have for us is important. We have arrived at the deepest point in the near-death experience—meeting that being who is or represents God. Yet for many experiencers, there is still more.

The Life Review

In this beautiful realm many experiencers are treated to a remarkable show called "The Life Review." It has been described as being in full color, three-dimensional, and shown as if on a wide screen. The review is extremely detailed and does not miss a thing. Some describe what looks like a slow-motion review, yet somehow their entire conscious lives are compressed into an astonishing reenactment of everything they have ever done. Such a review would take a long time in an earthly theater bound by time and space; yet within the few minutes of a near-death experience, the leading character is shown not only all the events of his or her former life, but can also experience the emotions that were involved. For example, a young man may not only see a time when he swiped a cake from a lunchbox, but he may relive the feelings he had about the incident. Even though the review is thorough, NDErs have not felt that someone has been recording their good and bad behavior or has been totaling up the score of their deeds to arrive at some eternal judgment about their lives.

The "life review" simply confirms Swedenborg's insight that all the moments of our lives are preserved in our memories. He was allowed to see the panoramic "life review," which shows what is meant by the "book of a person's life" mentioned in Revelation:

> It has been proved to me by manifold experience that when man passes from the natural world into the spiritual, as he does when he dies, he carries with him all his possessions, that is, everything that belongs to him as a man, except his earthly body . . . Moreover, a man's spirit enjoys every sense, both outer and inner, that he enjoyed in the world; he sees as before, he hears and speaks as before, smells and tastes, and when touched, he feels the touch as before; he also longs, desires, craves, thinks, reflects . . . Furthermore, he carries with him his natural memory, retaining everything that he has heard, seen, read, learned, or thought, in the world from earliest infancy even to the end of life.
>
> *Heaven and Hell* 461

Everything that happened during this life on earth in preparation for what is to come has become a part of us, and the images brought out during the life review can be quite damning:

> That when a man leaves the world he takes with him all his memory has been shown to me in many ways. . . . There were some who denied their crimes and villainies which they had perpetrated in the world. . . . All their deeds were disclosed and reviewed from their memory in order, from their earliest to their latest years.
>
> *Heaven and Hell* 462

It is a fearsome but easily believable list of evils. In Swedenborg's understanding, we will become exactly what our ideas and emotions during our life cause us to be. Many NDErs are able to see the acts that are still with them. Every detail of their lives has survived and will play a part in what lies ahead. In short, if we take into account these experiences, we will all judge ourselves! Every moment of our earthly life is subtly molding us, and we are forever changing—for better or for worse. At the moment of death, we are the product of all that has happened, and this has been inscribed on our "book of life."

Each person's book of life can be likened to a diary recorded in great detail. It is related to that vast memory record reflected in the NDE life review but is kept in everyone's personal library—even though each person seldom or never bothers to read it. Given today's technology, it also can be likened to a video recorder's capturing all of our experiences as they happen, not the way people whip out their video camcorder to preserve a child's astonishing achievements, but at a deeper level.

This particular diary, as planned by our infinitely wise and kind Creator, will actually be useful in making it possible for us to judge ourselves, rather than being hauled into a spiritual judge's court to debate our guilt or innocence. This diary is primarily a tool that makes it possible to look inside ourselves, to look into our motives and intentions as well as our acts, good or bad, that we have long forgotten. This is not for the purpose of dragging out past incidents, but primarily to have the opportunity to choose whether we really meant to do what we did and to decide whether or not we would do it again.

Swedenborg quotes the Bible extensively and makes many references to this so-called book of life, referring to it as the "remembrance of all the things that have been done, for everyone carries with him into the other life the memory of all his acts" (*Arcana Coelestia* 8620). Most of us, whether or not we want to admit it, have recorded in our book some pretty unpleasant chapters, hoping they would not become known.

Many elderly people say that life becomes meaningless as they get older, especially when they do not have a job. "What a waste of time," they say. But there is another way of looking at the subject. If we analyze our existence, we will find that there is always some thought that we've never had before. If we examine our thoughts or if we see something we have never seen before, this adds to our book of life. The longer a person lives, the more he or she can add to the book of life and the richer life becomes, if that person remains open to new experiences. All of our experiences play a part as we make new discoveries.

Many experiencers report this fascinating feature of being allowed to see the big picture. They were shown a vast cosmic view of creation and saw a logic, an order to their lives that made sense. One experiencer said, "When I saw the complete picture, I found myself saying, '*But of course, of course!*'" She finally understood how the many pieces of her life fit together.

The Barrier and Final Choice

Beyond the encounter with the radiant being of light, some experiencers progress into a beautiful spiritual realm, are shown a marvelous life-review, and finally come to the mystical "barrier." While NDE events do not clearly fall into a particular sequence, the "barrier" is always the final deciding event. In this final episode, progress is blocked. In many cases, it is a visible barrier such as a river, a fence, a gate, or a wall; but we can easily accept these as mere symbols. The experiencers have come to a point in their journey that will require them to make an important decision, something that, as we know, often happens during our lives.

Kenneth Ring, the most thoughtful scholar and NDE expert that I know, recently told me that, in his careful analysis of the NDE core experience, the person is only "near death" during the NDE until that highly significant last encounter, when he or she meets an "invisible barrier," or a gate, stream, fence, or wall. I agree with him that it is actually quite likely that a decision to *pass* that barrier would be the moment of death. This adds a dimension to the NDE that deserves further exploration and thought.

At this point, experiencers know that they are required to make a *choice*, to either go forward or to turn around. They are aware that, if they proceed in spiritual consciousness, they will move into a new setting and never recover from whatever injury, illness, or mishap triggered the near-death experience. Still, it is, for the most part, an opportunity with a choice; and many experiencers have reported that their decision to proceed or turn back was based on a feeling that there was something important in their earthly life still to be done: children to be raised, some task to be completed, or something else that needed their attention. The important thing to note is that the experiencers reported that they felt a certain freedom of choice in responding to the barrier.

Swedenborg, too, emphasized that a person's freedom is of primary importance. It is only the choices that individuals make in freedom that are a part of their true character. As we are well aware, life on earth is seldom really free. The pressures of everyday living that often affect our conduct, in one way or the other, do not determine our eternal welfare. Our ability to "choose," or to make a decision is what will really affect us. This remarkable choice in the near-death experience, when we are given the freedom to go one way or another, will greatly influence our lives.

Universally, NDErs report that they no longer have any fear of death, and nearly all experiencers report that they now believe in a life after death. Some effects are perplexing, such as in the case where the experiencer somehow becomes a psychic. Others gain the facility to heal people by the laying on of hands. Some report the ability to see an aura around other people. One IANDS survey of NDE after-effects asked the question, "Are you more or less religious since your NDE?" The majority of respondents answered that they felt more religious but went to church less frequently. We might say that, while their spiritual life increased, traditional religious institutions no longer met their needs.

Some experiencers have heard music, others have reported smelling sweet fragrances, and some had visions of deceased pets. As stated previously, no two experiences are the same; however, NDEs seem to follow a familiar pattern, in spite of the differences in detail, depth, and duration of the adventure. The sequence of the core experience might vary a great deal. Some NDEs are simple; others, complex— yet all are important. We know that the near-death experience for most is an ineffable experience and that it is something that will not be forgotten. It has none of the qualities of a dream, hallucination, or fantasy, and it has powerful effects on the lives of those who return.

However, those experiences when the person goes *beyond* the barrier are important because they represent the millions and millions of people who did not recover from their brush with death, whether or not they went through a dark tunnel or watched a life review. This implies that we are now talking about just about everyone who dies. I say "just about everyone" because there are vast cultural differences in what people believe about what happens after death. Regardless of what the cultural or religious background of people who die, however, they will go through the next-life experiences that are right for them.

Before Raymond Moody's *Life After Life* became a sensational bestseller, near-death experiences were, for the most part, a well-kept secret. Few people now doubt these astonishing accounts of a visit to a higher realm. The NDE may properly be considered to be a short visit to heaven.

§ **3** §

The Real World

Core experiences in the NDE scenario occur in a setting that we can accept or recognize as a spiritual
world. It is entirely unlike our familiar physical
world, not so much in its particular features as in its attrib-
utes. While those who find themselves in this beautiful
realm report that they see such things as mountains, hills,
meadows, forests, gardens, and even palaces and cities, they
speak of colors they have never seen on earth that are more
beautiful than they have ever experienced. The buildings or
cities seen in this realm are indescribably magnificent. But
surely the most important feature is that this world is peopled by other men, women, and children. Moreover, these
spiritual beings enjoy all their senses, only these are keener
than they have ever experienced in their earthly lives. As we
come into this marvelous living community, we also recognize one or more of these spirits. They are people we have
known, usually people we have loved. And most notable of
all, we are aware that these are friends who have previously
died, but who appear now to be in better physical condition
than ever.

Experiencers have made fascinating comments, such as
"I saw my grandfather, but he was no longer old and feeble";
"I saw Uncle Harry, but I noticed that he didn't limp

anymore"; "There was my grandmother, looking younger than I do." One experiencer received quite a shock. He reported that he recognized his good friend Al—but Al, he was sure, was still alive. The truth is that Al had died two weeks earlier, but his death was unknown to his friend. Al's death was verified when the NDEr told about his incredible experience! Indeed, in the spiritual realm, we meet old friends and loved relatives, and find them very much alive. There is an unmistakable message here about people who die. People who have lived on earth in the past are now "alive" in another realm, a wonderfully real world.

However, the NDE is an incomplete description of what we might experience in that spiritual realm. It includes a short visit into a new realm of consciousness, including beautiful descriptions and striking accounts of meeting deceased friends. But surely it does not reveal what will happen to us when we die. The NDE has been compared to a traveler's glimpse of a new city through the windows of the arriving train or plane—scarcely a complete experience. Swedenborg's works explore this new spiritual kingdom and its inhabitants, looking beyond the near-death experience.

The enormous amount of information about that world awaiting us is presented throughout Swedenborg's works, including information on how a spirit is "educated"—that is, brought to an understanding of earthly misconceptions about life after death. In *Conjugial Love* 9, he writes of some "newly arrived spirits" (people who had recently died) who are aware that they had left their previous life, and are eager to explore their new home. When asked, "What do you think heaven is like?" they respond that, in their life on earth, they had been promised that heaven would be something like "perpetual prayer and praising God." As these newly arrived spirits had been devoutly religious and had led good lives, they are admitted into a magnificent temple where they join the congregation in its happy expression of adoration. We can easily believe that, after several days of this sort of thing, the initiates become wearied and bored. When they try to leave, they cannot find an exit and realize that their "heaven" has become something less than happiness. Indeed, those from our earth with expectations that hell consists of fire, where erring humans are punished by God, also discover that they have been misled.

Swedenborg's explorations of this real world include highly detailed accounts of the afterlife. With his excellent training as a scientist and engineer, and his experience as the author of many scientific and philosophical books, he used the same thoroughness in describing his spiritual experiences. Being a careful observer with an eye for detail, he wrote conscientiously, meticulously cross-referencing paragraphs, and quoting extensively from the Hebrew Scriptures and the New Testament.

Swedenborg's spiritual writings, such as *Arcana Coelestia, Heaven and Hell*, and parts of *Apocalypse Explained* and *Apocalypse Revealed* provide a veritable geography of the heavenly worlds and fascinating descriptions of their inhabitants. His exploration of these worlds is truly remarkable, since his physical body remained in our natural world, often in his comfortable study. Even his housekeeper reported entering Swedenborg's room when he was apparently "out of this world" in a trance-like state, although he could be awakened and communicate when addressed.

Swedenborg also wrote personal notes and kept a diary of his excursions into the spiritual world. The *Spiritual Diary*, written between 1747 and 1765, includes long conversations with those he encountered and numerous descriptions of special visions he was shown in order to convey an important spiritual idea. For example, in *True Christian Religion* 508, he describes a vision in which he saw a temple in heaven with the Latin inscription *Nunc Licet*, which he states "signified that now it is permitted to enter understandingly into the mysteries of faith." The insights revealed to Swedenborg were not intended to be accepted on blind faith, but rather to be studied for a deeper comprehension of the spiritual truths they contain.

Realms in the Afterlife

During the twenty-seven years that Swedenborg moved in and out of the spiritual realms, he wrote extensively about what he saw and heard. His carefully detailed descriptions reach far beyond the near-death experience.

Swedenborg describes the spiritual world as having definite regions or "kingdoms," which are clearly divided into different parts—the natural, the spiritual, and the celestial or heavenly realms. In *Heaven and Hell*, Swedenborg describes the difference between the spiritual and the celestial realms and the relationship between them. Basically, he states that, within the spiritual heavens, people are primarily influenced by what they *know*, whereas, in the celestial or higher heavens, people are determined by what they *love*. The entire spiritual world is organized in a pattern comparable to the human body. Our human form is marvelously complex, in which each element has a special quality needed by the other parts, just as every tiny part of our bodies, external and internal, is essential for our overall wellbeing. With a little effort, we can come to see that there are individuals who have certain qualities that represent the countless organs and parts. There are spiritual counterparts even to ways of communicating.

NDErs have often reported that they communicated with the spirits they encountered, but not through verbal speech. It was an exchange of ideas unhindered by speech, in which the ideas themselves were far more important than mere words. Communication throughout the vast spiritual world is beyond the kind of speech we know.

Nonverbal speech can be called thought transfer. Who has not felt frustrated in trying to convey an important message in the inadequate and cumbersome words of any language? Describing the sunrise or sunset in a single word or groping for words to explain spiritual reactions to a certain piece of music can be difficult. In the spiritual world, however, thoughts and ideas are above and beyond simple symbols and can be conveyed to another person with great speed and clarity. In *Heaven and Hell* 248, Swedenborg states that "the speech of an angel or spirit flows first into a man's thought, and by an inner way into his organ of hearing, and thus moves it from within." This indicates that there is a joining of the two minds.

Another NDE feature reported by experiencers visiting another reality is that the spiritual realm is one in which there is no time or space. Through the early stages of the NDE, the experiencer is somehow free of time and space, floating through the tunnel and arriving in a beautiful realm. One experiencer said that she could see a group of people in the distance and wanted to find out who they were, so she *wished* she could be with them; and, suddenly, she found herself among the group, greeting old friends. Others have told how they moved from one place to another just by thinking about it. It goes beyond what Dorothy, in *The*

Wizard of Oz noted when she arrived in the Emerald City and said, "People sure do come and go quickly here!"

Swedenborg says that "thought brings presence." In other words, if we think about a person, he or she will then appear. It is also true that being close to another person in the spiritual realm really involves how similar or close we are to that person in our affections and ideas. This is often reflected by a group of people who come together simply because they care about the same things. It may not be easy to imagine this kind of proximity; yet, even in our own lives, we are often conscious of how we feel close to or separated from other people depending upon whether we share the same loves or ideas. To put it quite simply,

> Those are near to each other who are in like states, and those are at a distance who are in unlike states; and spaces in heaven are simply the external conditions corresponding to the internal states. For the same reason the heavens are distinct from one another, also the societies of each heaven and the individuals in each society.
>
> *Heaven and Hell* 193

Heaven is not one vast homogenous place, but is divided into a variety of groupings. In the spiritual world, there is a different kind of space. We can familiarize ourselves with such a realm by reminding ourselves of the ways in which our minds or thoughts are free to travel far beyond the tiny confines of our physical brain. In Swedenborg's terms, this first stage of life beyond death occurs in "the world of spirits," which is only one part of the spiritual world. The spiritual world includes the entire realm of the afterlife, and it has distinct parts; but the world of spirits is specifically the entranceway through which all humans pass. And this raises some important questions, especially for the nearly arrived spirit. The route through the world of spirits is a progression of choices, a spiritual journey that may take quite a long time. However, by the end of this journey, there will not be any doubt, even in the spirit's own mind, as to why it has come to a particular destination. The spirit comes to acknowledge its true love, its innermost intention, in order to arrive at its final destination, its eternal home. This home may be a heaven or a hell; but, as we shall see, this home is a place freely chosen by the spirit, not a reward or punishment. The term *judgment* has a whole new meaning.

Betsy Hoffman, one of the earliest and best-known experiencers, whose book *The Near-Death Experience* became a bestseller, said that, when she was told, "It is not yet your time," she asked, "But what about my sins?" The answer that was given to her has profound implications: "There are no sins here—not in the sense you mean it." Yet we know there are numerous transgressions against God's law. We can easily think of many individuals in history who have done horrible things; to put it very simply, we don't want to spend eternity in the same place with them.

The entire question of what we usually call "judgment" is unavoidable. If, for example, we think that we are going to spend eternity with people who are crooks, murderers, and thieves—it just would not be heaven. Far too many people in this life are evil and have freely chosen life patterns that make them undesirable companions. Swedenborg's view is straightforward: heaven is the place where people with good intent will go, and hell is the destination of those who prefer dishonesty, hate, ugliness, and cruelty.

Our behavior and actions, good or bad as they may be, are better understood as expressions of more important qualities. It is important to look beyond, or rather, *within* external actions to our internal motivations to determine the kind of people we really are.

A child raised in an environment where survival involves stealing and deception may well grow up to be a dishonest adult. But this behavior may not be *sin* in itself. From God's point of view, it is the motives or intentions behind such antisocial behavior that count. Thus, it would be unwise for us to judge someone born and raised in an unhealthy, dysfunctional family environment. It is not the evils one has committed during his or her lifetime that solely matter, but the evils one has come to love and would commit again in the spiritual world. These determine one's final destination, what will, as the Bible suggests, separate the sheep from the goats. This principle also applies to a vast array of evil activities that are not necessarily evident on the surface. Even unspoken words and inconspicuous actions that manifest hatred, greed, contempt, or blasphemy are sins, if we have made them our own by freely choosing them.

Ultimately, it is our internal motivation that determines whether or not we are good or bad people. The path between life on this earth and our eternal home involves a series of experiences, which not only make it possible for us to see ourselves as we really are, but present us with *free choices*, that is, choices with the external influences removed. Finally, it really comes down to a question of our *loves*. We will experience remarkable changes, when, in the spiritual world, we discover that our ideas of right and wrong could very well be mistaken. We will then learn what is truly right and be able to make a free choice. This process is pictured in Scripture as a judgment, and Swedenborg makes it clear that no one will be permitted to take any evils or falsities into heaven, nor will anyone take any truths or goods into hell. Many of the choices in this life involve our free decision as to which other spirits we will choose as our associates or friends. This spiritual "Ellis Island"—the world of spirits—ensures that nothing evil will go into heaven, as well as that nothing really good will go into hell where it will be perverted.

We arrive in the world of spirits complete, not only with all our memory from which we saw our "life review," but with all our loves and ideas also. Of course, we have a good many impure loves and false ideas, and these will not be expunged or eradicated by someone else. Instead, it will be up to us to choose which ideas and loves we wish to keep and which to reject.

The process of freely making choices is related to the life review since we will relive the decisions we have made during our life. This means that we will not necessarily take into heaven or hell some strange idea or weird fantasy from our youth, but we will be given the opportunity to re-experience the circumstances from the past and make a choice as to what to do.

As we make our choices, learn, and relive our worldly life, we will also be directed into the particular part of heaven or hell that reflects our loves and thoughts. This is a gradual, natural process; and, bit by bit, we will become the person we really are, since any pretense or hypocrisy will not stand up in this world where others can read our mind or where the sphere or aura around us reveals the type of person we are.

Each of us is quite different. The things we care about and what we think is true have been shaped during a lifetime, warts and all. We have acquired our habits and personalities over a long period of time, influenced by the situations in which we have lived, as well as by the company that we have chosen. We have developed our characteristics in ways over which we may have had limited, if any, control. So, in the spiritual world, we will tend to gravitate toward the place and the associates with whom we feel comfortable.

In addition to choosing to be among others like ourselves, we will follow directions that lead us to where our particular talents and delights enable us to express ourselves most freely in our relationships with other spirits. We will discover, if we do not already know it, that everyone in the spiritual world will use his or her particular talents and abilities to do things for others.

Most people try to find some sort of occupation or useful activity during this life on earth where they can somehow serve their neighbors. That is why architects are architects, entertainers are entertainers, policemen are policemen, and nurses are nurses. There are other uses in the spiritual world, including special ones that are almost beyond our comprehension. No one is idle or unemployed. In a similar way, we will find that we go where we belong. We find our way into the heaven or hell that matches our own special and unique character, moving into the particular home where we belong.

A Useful Life

Within both the spiritual and the celestial kingdoms, there are the equivalent of cities or towns (Swedenborg called them societies) where people come together who have the same kind of loves and the same ideas about spiritual subjects. This is not unlike our material world, with its great variety, except that there is harmony among those who live and work together in the heavenly societies. One of the clearest concepts throughout Swedenborg's books is that heaven is a kingdom of uses. "Uses" are ways in which angels can do something for other angels: they can use their talents and skills to contribute to the welfare and happiness of others. Imagine what it would be like to be in a community where all the inhabitants are harmonious, share the same loves and ideas, and find happiness in doing something good for each other. Isn't that heavenly?

Now, carry this idea to its opposite, to a realm where the spirits take their greatest delight in making each other miserable. This is hell. In the hells, spirits are permitted to do nasty things to each other, but are prevented from doing real damage, which is their frustration, vividly expressed in the idea of "hellfire." Hell is not a community of mutual usefulness. It is a place where behaviors do not contribute to the overall well-being of a community.

Would anyone actually choose evil and live in hell? Indeed, people do it all the time here on earth, often of their free choice. And this, obviously, is a wonderful aspect of the spiritual world. God provides that people *freely* go to where they feel they will be happy. Beyond that, they are given this choice even after they could have realized that they had made the wrong choice. The surprising message is that evil people prefer to be in hell, even in the particular hell they choose for themselves. But this does not suggest that hell is a pleasant ultimate destination.

While we are describing the progression to "where we belong," other changes will be happening. If we die when we are elderly, we find that we grow younger. If we had been plagued by ill health or physical limitations, we will become fit. If we die in childhood, we actually go through a development and "education" to reach the ideal situation for our unique qualities. This, of course, includes changing to become a better—or worse—spirit. Even the great number of people handicapped by physical or mental incapacities will have a new life in which they can learn about their real inner selves. They will not be hampered by their limitations, nor will they be able to get a free pass to heaven because of their earthly problems. It is also important to note that people who love each other will find each other and live together in happiness. This is actually a very complex and intricate process, but in the spiritual world we have the opportunity to choose freely to become the sort of spirit we want to be.

During the twenty-seven years that Swedenborg moved to and from the spiritual world, he provided abundant descriptions, but his descriptions reach far beyond the NDE, showing what may lie beyond the barrier that experiencers chose not to cross.

§ 4 §

Death and Near Death

Throughout the ages, a person's last moments have been clouded by fear and a host of ideas, from which have come many distorted beliefs. For a significant percentage of the population, their death may be their only activity that is reported in the local newspaper. And, of course, we are usually inundated with expressions about being laid to rest in the ground, in spite of a more important message from the New Testament, "He is not here! He is risen!"

The Rev. Chauncey Giles further illustrates this point in *The Nature of Spirit* (pp. 52–53) :

If death is the end of our individual and conscious being; if nothing remains but the ashes from the burnt taper, or a formless essence that soars away and mingles with the elements; if our glowing hopes, our lofty aspirations, our consciousness of capacities for knowledge and happiness which have just begun to expand, are all cut off by death, and buried in the grave,—then, indeed, man is the greatest enigma in the universe. . . . But if death is only the completion of the first little round of life, the first short flight; if it marks the end only of his seed time; of his budding hopes, his lofty aspirations, and dawning consciousness of desires which no earthly good can fill, are but the swelling germs of faculties that are to blossom and bear immortal fruit; if he leaves in the grave only the swaddling-clothes of his spiritual infancy, and rises as from a deep sleep, in perfect human form, with all his memory, his consciousness of individual being, to enter upon an endless career, in which hope is changed to fruition and aspiration into attainment, then death is the grand step in life.

Giles further explores what happens after the body reaches the limits of its capacities (p. 62):

The strength fails, the senses grow obtuse and dim; and the body becomes the soul's prison; shuts it out from the material world and all its delights; fetters its limbs with feebleness, and immures it in a dungeon, devoid of light and joy.

Giles ventures into a charming analogy as he addresses the question of somehow breaking out of this limiting physical body (66–68):

The plant and animal attain their perfection by distinct steps, and in the lower steps preparations are always made for the higher; and when the higher step is taken, the means by which it was taken become an encumbrance and are discarded. The natural world is full of illustrations of this law. . . . Take the sparrow in the egg, just before it bursts the walls of its prison and escapes into the air. Here is a fully organized being, and yet not one of its organs is adapted to its present condition. Here are bones, muscles, feathers, especially adapted, in every respect, to the air. every part is constructed with the utmost lightness, and the muscles are distributed and gathered into volume for the express purpose of giving strength where it is most needed. The form of the wing is made to cleave the air and bear the bird aloft. It has eyes for light, lungs for breathing, and a throat for song. But the sparrow can exercise none of these functions in the shell. Suppose it was conscious of its state as it lay there in its womb, but did not know of any other world than that in which it was dwelling. It feels the impulse to stretch its wings, and pour forth a song, but it has no scope for either. If it reasoned as many men do, it would say: "There is nothing here to content or satisfy me; but I know of nothing beyond. This shell is the boundary of my universe. If it should be destroyed, I might fall into nothingness, or be dispersed among the elements." . . .

Now, we believe that every bone and muscle and feather, every organ within and without, is a true prophet of its future state. We know also that every prophecy is fulfilled. These organs foretell another world of ineffable perfection compared with the one in which it was formed. They prophecy of air and light; of joyous song and social flight; of worms and seed for all its needs—and every prophecy is fulfilled to the letter.

It isn't the same without the excited prose of Chauncey Giles, but among the most frequent descriptions of the NDE is the expression "It was real!"

Maggie

In addition to the many opportunities I have had to meet with near-death experiencers and sit in on their discussions, as well as reading books and watching television shows about the NDE, I have been moved by hundreds of fascinating letters on this subject that were sent to me. In many cases, the letter was the first time that the writer's very personal experience had been shared. I have selected an example that includes features important to the understanding of the NDE and its effect on the experiencers.

I had known the woman I'll call "Maggie" thirty-five years ago, and it was a thrill to hear her voice again on the phone when she gave me permission to share part of her story. Maggie actually had two preliminary experiences, the first when she was eight years old in the process of having dental surgery: "As I was put to sleep, I saw my body rolled up like a ball and being hurled very fast through a long, dark tunnel."

Some years later she had her second preliminary experience, what she called a "vivid dream," which had several elements similar to the NDE:

I dreamed I was at the foot of a mountain. The mountain was bright and colorful. It almost looked like a confection, with wispy clouds floating about. There was a path leading around the mountain until it reached the top which was a beautiful place with tall spires penetrating the clouds, like shards of glistening glass.

Maggie was told, "We are not going all the way this time." She glanced at the beautiful place and knew immediately that "it was another existence. I turned reluctantly back down the path to the foot of the mountain. I awoke."

Some years later Maggie was admitted to the hospital with a pulmonary embolism. She recounts:

I was two months pregnant. I was given anticoagulants to dissolve the clot. I was told the massive doses of medicine

might cause me to abort. I said I would not. I carried my
baby to full term.

Immediately after giving birth, Maggie felt a certain strange-
ness; she told her husband, "The air is thick in my room;
something is hanging over us." A while later, when her baby
was brought to her, she suffered a massive pulmonary embolism. "I threw my sheets back and swung my legs out of
the bed, and I knew this was the time I had been waiting
for." A tremendous pain hit her suddenly, which was her last
conscious memory.

While unconscious, Maggie saw her husband and her
aunt nearby, though they did not reach the hospital until
later. She heard one of her doctors tell her, "You were gone
on the 15th, and something happened to you on the 17th,
which I do not understand. I did nothing to bring you back.
Some greater power than I did that." Her husband had been
called by a nurse's aide and told, "We lost Maggie." The aide
said that she had found Maggie with her eyes rolled back in
her head and that, if the husband wanted to see her again,
he must hurry.

Despite being unconscious, Maggie remained aware. "A
total blackness enveloped me, a blackness with no beginning
and no end, a total and complete blackness." Then she saw
herself on the floor beside her bed. A nurse was frantically
trying to help her and an orderly was dragging a large, or-
ange tank of oxygen into the room. The nurses were barking
orders to each other: "Call the Doctor!" "Call her husband!"
"Call a priest!" She was lifted onto the bed. Maggie could
hear the voice of a nurse at the nursing station, fifty feet
away, telling the doctor that the patient was dying.

When she had been put back into her bed, she did not
feel the mattress under her. "I was floating near the ceiling,"

she recalls, although no drugs had been administered. Her hearing became extremely acute; she heard (and saw) a patient in another room complaining about the moaning noise she heard coming from Maggie's room. But Maggie declares,

> I was feeling no pain. I felt wonderful. I felt like an observer, not a participant. I was just floating there between two worlds. One world I knew very well; the other I didn't know existed. To my right and above me the ceiling had given way to a path paved with blue-white clouds. The atmosphere seemed to be sprinkled with gold dust. It was very, very bright, and the light was blinding. I didn't see them, but I sensed the presence of many others and they were joyous. I, too, was joyous with anticipation of joining them.

Then, something caused her to look down into the room:

> Two doctors had arrived and they were with two nurses who were looking intently at a body on the bed. I took a long look at the body. It was a young woman in a yellow gown. She had very long hair, and it was damp, spread out on the pillow. Her eyes were tightly closed and drawn together. The lips were slightly opened and a smokey blue in color. She was not struggling to breathe and did not move at all.

Maggie saw another nurse and could read her thoughts, "It's too bad. She was only twenty-five"; and saw her leave the room, shaking her head to Maggie's husband, saying "I'm so sorry." Maggie heard further sad conversation and said, "I felt great sympathy for them. I tried to tell them I wasn't in pain. I wished they could be there with me." She could hear and see people in her room and in another room, wondering why "all of these people wanted me to come back and leave this wonderful place that I had found." She tried to tell them where she had been and made the decision to go back. "I gave a wistful look at the beauty of this other existence and started down, hovering over the body for a moment, thinking, 'I will go back up there another time.'" Returning, she immediately felt all the pain, felt the doctor pounding her chest with his fist, asking her how she felt. "I didn't feel anything up there. Now I hurt."

This somewhat shortened account illustrates many of the things we had described earlier: the black tunnel, the bright light, the beautiful realm and other spirits, and how, while out of her body, Maggie could see and hear what was happening around the empty body, which she didn't even recognize. As is always the case, there are differences in the details, but the pattern is strikingly like so many others. Maggie is a lovely woman I have come to know well, and her experience still moves me profoundly.

Children and the Near-Death Experience

Understandably, most reports of near-death experiences come from adults, even if the event itself happened many years earlier. Yet, a great many children have reported adventures into the mystical realm, and they have added interesting dimensions. *Closer to the Light*, written by pediatrician Melvin Morse, describes the NDE of a seven-year-old girl who had been found floating in an indoor pool. Dr. Morse was on duty at the hospital when the apparently dead little girl regained consciousness. He asked her, "What happened?" because he wondered how her drowning came about. She answered, "Do you mean before or after I sat on Jesus' lap?"

One survey indicated that 65% of children who have undergone near-death experiences mention the bright light. Nancy Evans Bush, president of IANDS and an investigator for the organization, collected experiences by children of different ages that she published in *Shades of the Prison-House Reopening*. In one episode, a four-year-old girl fell down a flight of cellar stairs because the light was not working. The child felt herself to be up near the ceiling and then noticed her own body lying on the cellar floor; she suspected that she was dead. Her experience included the familiar tunnel with a beautiful indescribable light, and she felt happier than she had ever been before or has ever been since.

Bush also recounts the story of a nine-year-old girl, fatally ill from a ruptured appendix, who provided an eloquent description of the beauty that followed the blackness:

> In its place was a beautiful soft pink light. All the weight was gone and I floated into the room as light as a feather. I seemed to be filled with this same light, which was the most profound spirit of love you can imagine.

A ten-year-old boy dying of an undiagnosed illness reported the following:

> I was in a dark tunnel. There was absolutely no sound and all was black. I was being wafted along as a speck of dust, but I felt at ease. I thought I was discovering a new cave.

He encountered a "sea of light," but he turned around because he felt that if he left the tunnel he would never find the light again. "I turned around and started back through the tunnel and that is the last I remember."

One of the NDEs reported by a young boy took place in an area I know well. The boy had been digging a tunnel in the sand during his family's visit to the New Jersey shore. His mother cautioned him not to make the tunnel too deep. The boy noticed a crack; suddenly, the sand caved in on him. He struggled, but the heavy sand prevented him from moving his body. The child was aware of a gleaming brightness, and he found himself traveling down a tunnel (not one of sand). While he was in the tunnel, visions from his young life flashed before him, such as when he came down the stairs at Christmas and saw the gleaming, lighted Christmas tree surrounded by gifts. He reports, "Then I saw my Mom and a man, and two other women. They were trying to dig me out. Now I knew I was dead." Later he came to the end of the tunnel and noticed "several people around a bright garden, but none of them had feet." He noticed a baby that he knew had drowned in a pool accident. He heard a voice say to him, "Struggle and you will live and return home," after which he woke up and found himself in the intensive care unit of a hospital. This boy ends his account with the pledge, "I will never dig any more tunnels again."

Another childhood NDE also occurred at the seashore. A woman tells of her experience twenty years earlier when she was seven years of age. She got caught in the surf and was thrashing around in panic when suddenly she felt total calm, a great feeling of peace. "The next thing is the most incredible and vivid memory of my life. I recall traveling or flying through a tunnel of immense brightness, at phenomenal speed." But the child was not scared. She met a man "of immense kindness, power, and love"; but he conveyed to her, without words, that she could not stay. She felt very distressed and abruptly found herself in the hospital. After her recovery, she says she had an "overwhelming interest in and love for Bible stories, though her family had no interest in religion."

We cannot tell directly what the youngest children and babies may experience of the other world. But among the most beautiful passages from Swedenborg are his descriptions of children in the afterlife, found in chapter 37 of *Heaven and Hell*. Young ones who die are given special attention by angels who have an abiding love for providing care and teaching children. Swedenborg assures us that in heaven there are no unwanted children; neither do they know pain nor sorrow. Indeed, children are permitted to grow and develop spiritually into angelhood.

The Role of Angels in the NDE

In recent years there has been increasing interest in and acceptance of those very special beings known as angels. Throughout the Bible, we read of angels communicating with people. Literature about the NDE includes numerous references to angels, although the first serious study of the subject did not come about until an article by Craig R. Lundahl was published in 1992 in the *Journal of Near Death Studies*. Personalities with angelic qualities were then reported as present in NDEs as guides or protectors; indeed, their participation is most impressive. One of the most familiar features of the NDE, "the being of light," could easily be interpreted as an angel. In several well-known instances, experiencers felt that an angel had come to assist them, even though not as pictured in great religious art with wings and halos.

Lundahl's article, "Angels in Near-Death Experiences," told of one NDEr who wrote, "My spirit left the body, and I could see it lying under the derrick. At that moment, my guardian angel, my mother, and my sister, were beside me. My mother died many years ago, my sister at the age of four years." In *Closer to the Light*, Melvin Morse noted that many children spoke of guardian angels being there to "escort them to heaven." One of the angels told the experiencer that he had been with him throughout the experiencer's life as a "guardian angel," and gave him instructions about what to do during his NDE. Lundahl's conclusion makes a lot of sense:

> In many NDEs, angels play a significant role in fulfilling the purpose of the NDE, especially in those instances where the NDEr encounters the other world. Although many people today no longer believe in the ministry of angels, there is evidence that they appear in NDEs and fulfill needed functions of guide, messenger and escort.

Swedenborg's descriptions of angels are strikingly different from the winged creatures we usually picture, but much more comfortable. Simply put, *all* good people become angels after death. Although they often need to go through a transition period in the world of spirits, when they reach their heavenly home, they are indeed angels. Not all angels, however, become involved welcoming newcomers who have just "awakened." Swedenborg observes in *Heaven and Hell*, quite logically, that there are certain angels who have a special love that qualifies them for this important assignment.

We all know people who were somehow born to take care of those in need. There are also those angels who welcome newcomers into the community. It is the kind of work that makes them happy. That's where they will have the greatest pleasure and will be appreciated by the newcomer.

The Negative Near-Death Experience

From the earliest discussion of what we now call NDEs, there has been an awareness that such experiences are not always ones of beauty, love, and light. These dark or negative near-death experiences paint a very different picture from the feelings of intense joy that most NDErs describe. Nevertheless, very few of these actually end in a negative way. Negative experiences nearly always end with something positive happening. After NDEs, people have a new sense of values or develop a different point of view. Our states of mind and what we are open to make a difference in all of our life experiences, including the NDE. In many cases, a negative NDE can change from something frightening into something blissful and beautiful. It is possible that the few negative NDEs on record are accounts of incomplete transitions from earthly to spiritual life.

I would inject a new way of evaluating the horrifying NDEs that occur. Terrifying experiences create their own imagery and symbolism—just as the symbols in a nightmare differ from those in a reassuring dream. We are most often not in a normal state of mind when we have these near-death experiences. If, for example, a woman "dies" in a dreadful highway accident, with screeching brakes, screams, and crashing vehicles, it would not surprise us if she experienced horrible visions, intense pain, or fear and terror about the situation. Remorse for a careless driving mistake, anger over a defect in the highway, or even the sudden awareness that she will never see her children again are negative circumstances that could be expected to spoil a beautiful or peaceful NDE. However, not every reported negative near-death experience has such obvious images. One well-known negative NDE was described as "ghastly" because the experiencer saw symbols like the yin-yang black-and-white curlicues: they flashed black and white, making a loud clicking noise. It was dreadful for the person experiencing it, but not necessarily something dreadful in and of itself. It was the person's state of mind that made it a bad experience. Such an experience may be attributed to an incomplete NDE.

Beyond the NDE, our consideration of the life after death has emphasized the beauty, love, and happiness awaiting us. But the subject would be insufficient if we ignore the reality of hell. *Heaven and Hell*, Swedenborg's best-known book, presents the subject of "damnation" in ways far different from those generally held in other major religions. After all, religions that teach the importance of being good also must warn that being bad will result in highly unpleasant punishments.

Swedenborg's conception of hell contrasts to the traditional vision of those "lakes of hell" filled with fire and brimstone, tended by devils with pitchforks and nasty dispositions, and the idea that God will eternally punish every evildoer. In Swedenborg's understanding, there is no "Devil," and the Lord is pure love and mercy. God never takes vengeance on people, even when it might be richly deserved.

Some folks react strongly against this idea. They feel

that it just would not be fair if a thug responsible for a crime were allowed to go unpunished by God. Even though the fear of God's punishment and a thoroughly unpleasant hell are useful in guiding our behavior, such a belief simply does not guarantee our salvation. We should avoid evil *not* because we do not want to suffer for our sins, but because we hate bad behavior and love God.

In its simplest expression, the concept of a loving, merciful God who condemns no one seems to be in conflict with many sincere Christian teachings that denounce evildoers and their sins. It is easy to quote passages from the Bible that warn of dire consequences when we stray from the straight and narrow path. The fear of punishment or the torments of hellfire, however, do not transform a bad person into a good one, since such a person wishes to commit crimes in his or her heart, where the intention is most prominent. Sometimes, people have been caught in situations they did not choose to be in or have made errors that they deeply regret; their intention will be the basis for the judgment.

As we have seen previously, in Swedenborg's descriptions, not everyone who arrives in the afterlife is a transformed being ready for heaven. With the exception of infants who have died before they could make life choices, people who awaken into the world of spirits begin the important process whereby they put off their bad habits and ideas or choose to live in a more hellish state. The length of time it takes to make the free choice of heaven or hell may vary considerably. During that indefinite period, the newly deceased are reliving memories of life on earth, rejecting those qualities they now dislike or confirming any really bad tendencies. They do this to a great extent by freely associating with spirits who have the same desires, tendencies, and loves as they do.

This is clearly a more involved process than the simple concept of going "up" to heaven or "down" to hell. Swedenborg's concept of the heavens and hells involves searching out the things we find pleasant, associating with kindred spirits like our old friends. Heaven and hell are filled with a variety of different loves and ideas. We can choose our final homes and find ways to be of use in a way that is remarkably similar to our natural tendency to seek out friends who agree with us. We can discover eternal places that reflect our unique tastes and preferences.

Living with a Changed Attitude

Those of us working in the NDE field have become aware of a tremendous change in the public's feelings about these amazing experiences. We had worked hard, years before, to convince our audiences that the NDE was real. Many people displayed their skepticism and doubts, but attitudes have changed. Maybe as the result of numerous television reports and re-enactments, a large general audience has become familiar with the OBE, the dark tunnel, the being of light, the beautiful realm, and the life review. Many questions remain, but the situation today feels unmistakably different.

The surge of interest in the near-death experience arising from Moody's *Life after Life* could have peaked in the past twenty years as the public turned its attention to other interests. But it is significant that the near-death experience continues to attract public attention at an astonishing rate. Indeed, public interest in the near-death experience has expanded to include other spiritual elements in our lives. The overall effect has gone far beyond the NDE itself. The subject of the NDE opened up a willingness to listen to and talk about spiritual experiences and paranormal subjects. An astonishing interest in the subject of angels, as well as other experiences such as spirit communications, continues to develop. These subjects would not have been openly discussed prior to the mid-1970s.

Such shifts in public perception have appeared before. Our ancestors' lives were enormously influenced by ideas of unseen forces that could control people's destiny. Today, we largely reject the notion of fate or of life based solely on chance or the whims of arbitrary gods. And, fortunately, we no longer burn witches. But many Pennsylvania "Dutch" farmers still make sure that there is a hex sign on their barns; and people from all walks of life still cross their fingers for protection, do not walk through cemeteries at night, pick up pennies ("heads-up" only) to assure good luck, and take special care to avoid danger on Friday the thirteenth. Did you ever "knock on wood"; look for four-leaf clovers; carry a rabbit's foot; or avoid breaking mirrors, crossing the path of a black cat, or walking under ladders? Other cultures may have different or similar recognitions of unseen forces. Such superstitions are not held in high regard in our age of science and reason, and most of us have long progressed beyond the simple beliefs of our ancestors.

We have long been familiar with innumerable religious visions reported throughout the ages, and newspapers continue to report other encounters, such as children experiencing a vision of the Virgin Mary. How all these experiences relate to the NDE is not always clear, but they do affirm the reality of a world filled with spirits.

As a Swedenborgian, I have always felt that our understanding of life after death was quite rational, even though it involved a belief in unseen spirits and angels. This change in attitude about dying is quite significant because what we believe lies ahead, our final destiny, affects the way we live our lives. If belief in the afterlife, especially a life that makes sense, shapes our moral values and our beliefs about God's providence, the increase in public acceptance of a logical life after death will modify human behavior in highly favorable ways. No matter what our religious background, if we examine our conduct and carefully choose to avoid destructive actions and thoughts, and if we love other people, we will behave in the ethical manner that most religions have always promoted.

In an article entitled "The Impact of Near-Death Experiences on Persons Who Have Not Had Them," published in the summer 1995 issue of the *Journal of Near-Death Studies*, Kenneth Ring reports on his study of nonexperiencers who have merely heard or read about the NDE, and finds that these accounts significantly changed their attitudes. These vicarious NDEs did not include any supernatural experience, but resulted in positive images on the subject of death and dying and the prospects beyond death.

Those who have experienced the higher realm of consciousness find that their lives have been greatly changed, and nearly always there has been an observable improvement. Experiencers do not rush back into religious organizations that they have neglected, and most experiencers would probably agree that religious denominations have very little to say about the life after death. Even the Bible says surprisingly little about what lies beyond the grave. All the wonderful art and literature of the world religions simply does not compare to what people experience themselves when they suddenly see the spiritual reality. I suspect that very few artists were experiencers.

Yet a man who may scarcely remember even the most vivid dreams will unhesitatingly declare that his NDE was real and has greatly affected his life. As I reported earlier, the majority of NDErs come back from their adventure with a renewed sense of being put on the earth for a purpose. Their dedication is often bolstered by the fact that they no longer fear death. It seems that the awareness of life after death influences the understanding of life before death.

⸕ 5 ⸕

Unanswered Questions

Though tremendous progress has been made in the past two decades, there is a great deal we do not yet know about the near-death experience. Quite a few talented researchers have devoted time and attention to this fascinating subject, but there is so much we still have to learn.

We do not understand why people are largely unaware of the higher level of consciousness until they are badly hurt. In fact, they have to be almost killed to develop this insight. The narrow slit that opens to allow this astonishing view into the vast realm of spiritual existence is not something to be taken lightly. Some people who have had a near-death experience found it so marvelous that they have toyed with the idea of recapturing that blissful, beautiful, glorious moment. It is understandable that attempts have been made to recreate the NDE or to set up controlled situations in which it is possible to approach death and then reverse the process before it is too late. The truth is that this is a very serious matter, and people are simply not wise enough or reliable enough to indulge in this kind of experimentation.

Although there is limited research of this type, I do not believe we will ever reach the point where we can conduct controlled laboratory tests in which the process of dying is stopped just before death takes place. Moreover, laboratory conditions are difficult to simulate in ways comparable to dying from drowning, a highway collision, strangulation, shootings, surgery, childbirth, or being hit by lightning.

Other questions are equally elusive. I have wondered for years just why it is that we have no accounts of simultaneous NDEs. By this, I mean a situation in which a small or large group of people are brought just to the brink of death at the same time, in the same place. We need to have a situation where the experiencers will be returning to tell us about it. Perhaps we could examine near-fatal drownings instead. But it would have to be multiple drownings, such happened in the great Johnstown, Pennsylvania, flood of 1889, where the dam broke and emptied the artificial lake on the town in the valley.

There are some NDE accounts where several people were involved, but I have never learned about one where the experiencer saw or was conscious of other people sharing and undergoing the same experience at the same time, such as an instance where several people enter the now-familiar tunnel at one time. It would be fascinating to study a simultaneous NDE disaster. If an airplane crashed and the passengers "died" at the same instant, this experience would probably be comparable to one when an airplane lands at the terminal and all the people go their own ways.

Perhaps the lack of a group NDE means that each person's experience of spiritual life is unique. I would not expect those involved in a personal experience to be particularly aware of other people undergoing the same experience. Just being in the same place at a given point in time does not mean that we are *spiritually* in the same place. Many victims of the terrible bombing of the Murrah Federal Building in Oklahoma City in 1995 reported near-death experiences, but they did not share the same NDEs. Each of us is special in the eyes of God, and each of us will have his or her own experience in the spiritual world. Perhaps someday we will learn of people who actually shared a near-death experience, and I often wonder if they will be identical twins.

A person might die as an infant, a teenager, or an octagernarian. That moment of dying affects people so profoundly that their entrance into the spiritual world might be at exactly the right time for their eternal welfare. The testimony of many NDErs suggests that some occasions are more appropriate than others for passing into the spiritual world.

The study of NDEs can lead to a different way of thinking about an untimely death. Though we think of a good full life carrying us beyond "three score years and ten," God allows us to die at the point when we have the greatest opportunity for eternal happiness. If we were spared and lived beyond our time, because of advances in medical science or other events, we might well encounter circumstances for which we are not prepared, and possibly our eternal welfare could be adversely affected.

Parents know that it is sometimes necessary to discipline the children they love, to deny them something or sometimes to punish them for some wrongdoing. Though children are aghast at these edicts, and sometimes rebel against them, our discipline is mainly intended for their welfare. In a similar way, the NDE and many universal lessons give us a glimpse of God's infinite power and infinite wisdom. God loves us and unceasingly works to assure our happiness, even when we resist.

Other Paranormal Experiences

As recently as two decades ago, an appreciable majority of those we may consider to be the educated population felt enlightened enough to scoff at ghosts, disparage spirit voices, chuckle at angels and devils, and accept the reality and finality of death when it comes. Yet over and over again, we find that humanity throughout recorded history has never been really that enlightened. The Bible is full of unbelievable events and activities, and ancient legends and architectural ruins tell us in countless ways that our ancestors took the unseen world very seriously. Much of the physical evidence from past civilizations has been studied by highly educated scholars. They attempt to make sense of the Egyptian "spirit door" or an ancient, elaborate embalming process, but there is much that remains unexplained. On Easter Island in the South Pacific, there are awesome stone statues, some six hundred eyeless human figures grouped on sacred platforms. How they were carved or transported many miles to their location remains a mystery. Just about everywhere, we find evidence that human beings have been highly motivated by beliefs that would not appeal to many people in the twentieth century.

But beliefs in the occult have been persistent and universal, and cannot be lightly dismissed. The biblical miracles and prophecies, the countless legends among ancient people, and a wide spectrum of psychic experiences present an impressive collection of material that attests to a world beyond our present material existence.

In addition, peak experiences, hypnogogic states, and a vast spectrum of dreams and visions have impressed many spiritual seekers. There have indisputably been charlatans and frauds, ranging from carnival card readers and mind readers to psychics such as Nostradamus. In the case of Nostradamus, his visions of what was going to happen were couched in words and ideas that could be interpreted in many ways. There are plenty of false prophets in our world and we need to be cautious of their predictions. Despite this, many of us have had visions, insights, or strangely predictive hunches. The human mind is far too intricate and amazing to brush aside the continuing parade of psychic anomalies. Visions or psychic events may not involve a close brush with death, but there is a message to be found in these paranormal experiences. That message is simple: a real and affecting spiritual world surrounds us all the time.

Millions who have experienced NDEs have seen and heard things that cannot be explained. But no matter how fantastic the experience, there is an impressive consistency in NDE explorations of a higher realm, as well as a great many examples of things NDErs have learned that cannot otherwise be explained. Even though we do not see or hear them, there are always spirits around us. This wonderful interplay between spirits and people is revealed in people's visions, inspirations, and flashes of genius, as well as in their changing moods and passions.

We can make sense out of the idea that people can become "possessed" by evil spirits, driven to commit heinous crimes, as a legal defense of insanity attests. A crowd, too, can become possessed, as in the angry passion of a mob bent on lynching; or an entire population following an evil leader can be swept away, obediently committing horrors in his name, as we have witnessed all too frequently in our own century.

But people can also be influenced by good and noble ideas and put them into action in their lives on a very personal level. Examining ourselves, seeking out our real

motives, or deciding to tell an obsessing spirit, "Get thee behind me!" are positive internal decisions we can make.

Though I believe we are surrounded and deeply influenced by the spirits around us, I do not try to seek contact
with them. Swedenborg warned in *Heaven and Hell* 249 that
disorderly spirits may respond if we seek to make contact
with the spiritual world. I have heeded that warning. The
use of mediums and seances to communicate with departed
loved ones can be very dangerous. The world of spirits is a
very real world, but one to be approached with care.

The Divine Plan

Swedenborg believed that God, who is the very essence of
love, or love itself, created the universe in order to bestow
on us the blessings of a happy eternal life. God does not
compel people to be good, and their true happiness depends
on their own choosing to obey. God's intent is to provide all
the opportunities in the natural world needed for us to develop into angels who can live eternally in heaven. This includes all people everywhere—even the most primitive and
isolated people on this earth—and this has been true
through countless ages. It is quite remarkable that God per-
mits a wide range of ideas in order to keep alive humankind's belief in something beyond our mere mortal
existence. It is better for people to think of returning to another life than to believe that death will be the final end. It
is my personal conviction that the entire phenomenon of
the near-death experience is a part of the vast divine plan to
assure our best possible destiny.

The most difficult concept of the near-death experience

concerns the moment when so many experiencers reach that point, at the barrier, where they are actually given the choice either to go on or to return. What could be so important that someone would choose to return to this life? Those who tell us about such choices have their many reasons, including "to take care of my children," "to care for my elderly mother," "to finish that project I've been working on." Such concerns, indeed, may be involved, but it is highly likely that their return and recovery after a glimpse into a higher existence is for more reasons than they can scarcely comprehend.

Everything that happens to any individual or to humanity as a whole is, in the divine plan, intended to serve the greatest happiness. This means that there was a *reason* for thirteen million people to have had a near-death experience, that great adventure into a higher realm of consciousness. Each one of them, in his or her unique way, was playing a part in the progression of human consciousness from a primitive knowledge to an increased understanding of God's purpose for humanity. The experience itself transformed them, changed them into wiser and better people. In addition, it had an impact on all of the people around them. Something of tremendous importance happened to the sick or injured person on the threshold of eternity, but also to other people, including the close relatives and loved ones who would have profoundly grieved over the experiencer's death.

It is reasonable to assume that many of the publicized NDEs have affected hundreds of others. In each instance, there was learning or discovery, often with a great deal of emotional involvement. The result has been that significant portions of the public have also been transformed by individual NDE stories, even if the experiencer had been a total stranger. Many NDE books have become bestsellers, which means that thousands of men and women are intrigued by this subject. Many people have attended lectures or work-shops because they have felt that there was a message for them in another person's brush with death. Clearly, the human family has undergone a spiritual change in the past twenty or thirty years that could have a profound effect on all of us.

But why is this wide-spread knowledge about NDEs so important? The answer is not a simple one. But if we think about it with an open mind, there are startling implications for the human race and for each of us.

People are free to accept or reject God's love, since few would attempt to deny that, if they were forced to love someone, they would not really love that person. The vast process of learning to know and love our Creator cannot be hurried. We get a glimpse of this when we take into consid-eration the tiny infants born into our care, and the slow process in which they eventually can come really to love their parents.

The biblical story of Genesis, deceptively simple, is full of wisdom. In the Garden of Eden, Adam disobeyed the di-vine command that he was not to eat of the tree of the knowledge of good and evil even though it was "good for food and pleasant to the eye." The seductive serpent assured Eve that she and Adam would not die as God had said. When they ate of the fruit of the forbidden tree "their eyes were opened." They did not die physically, yet they did die spiritually, their disobedience resulting in their expulsion from the beautiful paradise.

Concepts contained in the New Testament literally al-tered human thought and values and changed much of the world, without weapons. This includes examining the beliefs held through the centuries about witches, magic, sorcery and strange, tyrannical gods. Passing centuries have ushered in great ages of artistic achievements and intellectual en-lightenment. Undoubtedly, near-death experiences have oc-curred throughout the ages, but it is likely that most experiencers kept quiet about them rather than be ridiculed and have their sanity doubted. Currently, Western culture is more receptive to the NDE phenomenon. People are becom-ing more informed about spiritual wisdom, and information about NDEs is more easily shared than in the past.

The burst of interest following Moody's *Life After Life* can be largely attributed to the fact that there were many who had "died" and "recovered" with a strong belief in a dif-ferent existence. When they found published and credible assurance that they were not alone, they gladly came out of the closet. As early experiencers went out to share their sto-ries, they expected and received vigorous skepticism. They were told that these hallucinations were the result of med-ications, oxygen deprivation, self-hypnosis, or endorphins. It was, of course, the experts—doctors, psychologists, clergy, and others—who were the most resistant. Yet the NDE sim-ply would not be denied. The NDE was real enough to the experiencers, but how could nonexperiencers understand this adventure or accept its reality?

Dreams are real to the dreamer. There are many people who take dreams quite seriously, but experiencers uniformly insist that the NDE is not a dream. Experiencers have told me, "It was more real than you are," "It was the most real thing I've ever been through," and—unlike many dreams—the NDE is remembered in great detail.

During the near-death experience, millions of people did not just have pleasant (and a few unpleasant) visions. They insist that, while their lifeless body lay quietly there, they could *see* that body (with its eyes closed) and watch the people around that body and hear what they were chatting about. They felt that they had been "drawn out of" that body and were now floating above it, feeling fine! They tell of passing through that dark tunnel, approaching an indescribable and ineffable light, and entering a beautiful new realm, peopled by other spirits, often recognized as friends. If such things are vehemently described as "real," we must adjust our concept of reality.

What is the Message?

Considering the history of humanity's intellectual development, it is apparent that people frequently change their minds about many things. What was believed at one time can be questioned, and we can look at many subjects again from a different viewpoint. The message of the near-death experience is one of the profound awakenings of the ages.

Consider that message in its simplest form. The living beings who have accomplished so much—the experiencers—were liberated by the process most of us mistakenly think of as the end. The *real* person survives those apparently fatal diseases and injuries that stop the breath and beating heart. People survive death!

This is a revolutionary concept because we begin to realize that the wondrous human body is a complex machine intended to serve people for a finite number of years, then to be cast aside. But those years allotted to us are given in order to prepare us for the "real world" by educating us in ways comparable to what many people preparing to move to a new country would do.

From all we have examined through the near-death experience, we can be assured that the actual experience of dying is not what it appears to be, although it is not something to be prematurely invited, since there is real purpose to this earthly life. The transition to the next life is described with glowing terms: peaceful, painless, restful, and calm. Then we are told of things that cannot be adequately described, the ineffable feeling of peace, love, and caring.

As the drama begins to unfold, we are released from our physical bodies so that we can observe the situation we will leave behind us—the frantic friends or methodical medics—and we are aware that their concern for the vacated body is commendable, but it is rather unimportant to us. We are tempted to communicate with them because, astonishingly, we have keen sight and can hear and understand their conversations. We are not distressed by being suspended above the scene and may even enjoy the floating sensation, finding ourselves next hurtling through a tunnel of darkness—black because we do not comprehend what is happening. But then, up ahead, there is a golden light, a welcoming sight; and we sense that we will soon know more. And the light, now brilliant but not blinding, can convey ideas to us. It is not merely an incandescence, but a caring, profoundly wise and loving personality. Even though its message may be that we have arrived ahead of schedule, we may next progress into a realm, beautiful beyond words, with sights and colors to delight us, a magnificent place inhabited with other people, very much alive. We recognize loved ones and friends. The symbolic barrier we encounter offers us a choice, for we are still ourselves, still empowered to make decisions as to what is important.

There are so many fascinating questions, so much to learn. I find myself remembering Kenneth Ring's invitation: if you have any questions to ask, if you have any stories to tell, then, "Come up here!"

Appendix
Swedenborg and the Core Experience
compiled by Wendell Barnett

Although the spiritual journeys of Emanuel Swedenborg were not near-death experiences, his descriptions of the afterlife provide parallels to standard features of the NDE core experience. The following is a collection of excerpts from Swedenborg's works, grouped under features of the near-death experience that have been noted by leading NDE researchers.

Ineffability

A certain good spirit, was taken up into the first heaven, and speaking with me from thence he said that he saw infinite things in what I was then reading in the Word; when yet I myself had only a simple thought on the subject. Afterward he was taken up into a more interior heaven, and he said from thence that he now saw still more things, and so many from thence that he now saw still more things, and so many that what he had seen before were comparatively gross to him. He was next taken up into a heaven still more interior, where the celestial angels are, and he said from thence that what he had before seen was scarcely anything compared with the things he now saw.

Arcana Coelestia 6617

The wisdom of angels is indescribable in words, it can only be illustrated by some general things. Angels can express in a single word what a man cannot express in a thousand words.

Heaven and Hell 269

For this reason their speech is so full of wisdom that they can express in a single word what man cannot express in a thousand words; also the ideas of their thought include things that are beyond man's comprehension, and still more his power of expression. This is why the things that have been heard and seen in heaven are said to be ineffable, and such as ear hath never heard nor eye seen.

Heaven and Hell 239

The delights of heaven are both ineffable and innumerable; but he that is in the mere delight of the body or of the flesh can have no knowledge of or belief in a single one of these innumerable delights . . . for these so extinguish and suffocate the interior delights that belong to heaven as to destroy all belief in them.

Heaven and Hell 398

The universal heaven is a heaven of love, for there is no other life in the heavens than the life of love. From this is derived all heavenly happiness, which is so great that nothing of it admits of description, nor can ever be conceived by any human idea.

Arcana Coelestia 32:2

As regards the paradisal scenes, they are amazing. Paradisal gardens are presented to view of immense extent, consisting of trees of every kind, and of beauty and pleasantness so great as to surpass every idea of thought; and these gardens are presented with such life before the external sight that those who are there not only see them, but perceive every particular much more vividly than the sight of the eye perceives such things on earth. . . . Certain souls, new-comers from the world—who from principles received while they lived, doubted the possibility of such things existing in the other life, where there is no wood and stone—being taken up thither and speaking thence with me, said in their amazement that it was beyond words, and that they could in no way represent the unutterableness of what they saw by any idea, and that joys and delights shone forth from every single thing, and this with successive varieties. The souls that are being introduced into heaven are for the most part carried first of all to the paradisal regions.

Arcana Coelestia 1622:1, 2

Serenity

He who is being resuscitated is in a tranquil state, being still guarded by the celestial angels.

Arcana Coelestia 184

Afterwards. . . perception is communicated to him, the angels being especially cautious to prevent any idea coming from him but such as is of a soft and tender nature, as of love; and it is now given him to know that he is a spirit.

Heaven and Hell 185

As man is unable, as long as he is in the body, to receive the peace of heaven, so he can have no perception of it, because his perception is confined to what is natural. To perceive it he must be able, in respect to thought, to be raised up and withdrawn from the body and kept in the spirit, and at the same time be with angels. In this way has the peace of heaven been perceived by me; and for this reason I am able to describe it, yet not in words as that peace is in itself, because human words are inadequate, but only as it is in comparison with that rest of mind that those enjoy who are content with God.

Heaven and Hell 284

Joy

I had also in my mind and in my body as it were a sensation of an indescribable delight, so that if it had been more intense, the body would have been as it were dissolved from the delight alone.

Journal of Dreams 48

Noise

About twelve, one, or two o'clock in the night there came over me a very powerful tremor from the head to the feet, accompanied with a booming sound as if many winds had clashed against one another. It was indescribable, and it shook me and prostrated me on my face. In the moment that I was prostrated I became wide awake, and I saw that I had been thrown down. I wondered what it meant, and I spoke as if I were awake, but still I found that the words were put into my mouth, and I said, "Oh, Thou Almighty Jesus Christ, who of Thy great mercy deignest to come to so great a sinner, make me worthy of this grace!" I kept my hands folded and I prayed, and then there came forth a hand which strongly pressed my hands. . . . I perceived that it was the Son of God Himself who descended with such a resounding noise which by itself prostrated me to the ground, and that it was He who effected the prayer and thus declared it to be Jesus Himself.

Journal of Dreams 52–53; 55

The Out-of-Body Experience

Especially was I permitted to see and feel that there was a pulling and drawing forth, as it were, of the interiors of my mind, thus of my spirit, from the body; and I was told that this is from the Lord, and that the resurrection is thus effected.

Heaven and Hell 499

First, as to withdrawal from the body, it happens thus. Man is brought into a certain state that is midway between sleeping and waking, and when in that state he seems to himself to be wide awake; all the senses are as perfectly awake as in the completest bodily wakefulness, not only the sight and the hearing, but what is wonderful, the sense of touch also, which is then more exquisite than is ever possible when the body is awake. In this state spirits and angels have been seen to the very life, and have been heard, and what is wonderful, have been touched, with almost nothing of the body intervening. This is the state that is called being withdrawn from the body, and not knowing whether one is in the body or out of it. I have been admitted into this state only three or four times that I might learn what it is, and might know that spirits and angels enjoy every sense, and that man does also in respect to his spirit when he is withdrawn from the body.

Heaven and Hell 440

As man's spirit means his mind; therefore "being in the spirit" (a phrase sometimes used in the Word) means a state of mind separate from the body; and because in that state the prophets saw such things as exist in the spiritual world it is called a "vision of God." The prophets were then in a state like that of spirits and angels themselves in that world. In that state man's spirit like his mind in regard to sight, may be transferred from place to place, the body remaining meanwhile in its own place. This is the state in which I have now been for twenty-six years, with the difference that I am in the spirit and in the body at the same time, and only at times out of the body.

True Christian Religion 157

One morning most sweet singing, heard at some height above me, woke me from sleep; and in that first vigil, which is more internal, peaceful, and sweet than the following hours of the day, I was enabled to be kept for some time in the spirit, as if out of the body, and could give exquisite attention to the affection which was being sung.

Conjugial Love 155[2]

Jehovah himself spoke the Word through the prophets. We read of the prophets that they were in vision, and that Jehovah spoke to them. When they were in vision they were not in the body, but in their spirit, in which state they saw things such as are in heaven. But when Jehovah spoke to them, they were in the body, and heard him speaking. These two states of the prophets should be carefully distinguished. In their state of vision, the eyes of their spirit were opened, and those of their body shut, and they then seemed to themselves to be carried from place to place, the body remaining in its own place.

Conjugial Love 52, 63

Reunions

The state of man's spirit that immediately follows his life in the world being such, he is then recognized by his friends and by those he had known in the world; for this is something that spirits perceive not only from one's face and speech but also from the sphere of his life when they draw near. Whenever any one in the other life thinks about another, he brings his face before him in thought, and at the same time many things of his life; and when he does this the other becomes present, as if he had been sent for or called.

Heaven and Hell 494

Angels and spirits, or men after death, when permitted by the Lord, can meet all whom they have known in this world, or whom they have heard of—whomsoever they desire—can see them as present, and can converse with them. Wonderful to say, they are at hand in a moment and are most in intimately present; so that it is possible to converse not only with friends, who usually find one another, but also with others that have been respected and esteemed.

Arcana Coelestia 1114

When those who are in the other life first enter it, . . . they also retain in mind the companions they have had in the life of the body, and it is then permitted by the Lord that they also find them and speak with them as on earth, yet no otherwise than is permitted or granted them. Thus everyone can find his friends, parents, and children, but still they can remain there together no longer than is granted them by the Lord.

Spiritual Diary 610

I have not only been informed by the angels that such is the case, but I have also spoken with a certain one who had died when an infant, and yet then appeared as an adult. The same also spoke with his brother who had died in adult age, and this from so much mutual brotherly love that his brother could not refrain from tears, saying that he perceived no otherwise than that it was love itself that was speaking.

Arcana Coelestia 2304

The Being of Light

Afterwards, . . . he then commences his life. This at first is happy and glad, for he seems to himself to have come into eternal life, which is represented by a bright white light that becomes of a beautiful golden tinge, by which is signified his first life, to wit, that it is celestial as well as spiritual.

Arcana Coelestia 185

I have also seen the Lord out of the sun in an angelic form, at a height a little below the sun; also near by in a like form, with shining face, and once in the midst of angels as a flame-like radiance.

Heaven and Hell 121e

On one occasion, awakening from sleep I fell into a profound meditation about God; and looking up I saw above me in heaven an exceedingly bright light of oval form; and as I fixed my gaze upon it the light withdrew to the sides and formed a circle; and then, behold, heaven opened to me.

True Christian Religion 25:1

Such is the light in the heavens that it exceeds by man degrees the noonday light of the world. . . . The brightness and splendour of the light of heaven are such as cannot be described.

Heaven and Hell 126

After a person comes into the sensation of eternal life, he feels quite pleasant and happy. This was represented to me by a beautiful bright yellow light by which is signified his first life, namely that it is celestial and spiritual.

Spiritual Diary 1117

The sun of heaven is the Lord; the light there is the Divine truth and the heat the Divine good that go forth from the Lord as a sun. . . . In heaven the Lord is seen as a sun, for the reason that he is Divine love, from which all spiritual things, and by means of the sun of the world all natural things, have their existence. That love is what shines as a sun.

Heaven and Hell 117

In the lowest or first heaven, the Lord does not appear as a sun . . . , but only as a light which far surpasses the light of the world.

Arcana Coelestia 6832:2

Life Review

This shows what is meant by the book of man's life spoken of in the Word, namely, that all things that he has done and all things that he has thought are inscribed on the whole man, and when they are called forth from the memory they appear as if read in a book, and when the spirit is viewed in the light of heaven, they appear as in an image . . . never obliterated, . . . never erased.

Heaven and Hell 463

Such therefore is the interior memory that there are inscribed on it all the single, nay, the most singular things that the man has ever thought, spoken, and done; nay, even those which have appeared to him as but a shade, with the minutest particulars, from his earliest infancy to the last of old age. The memory of all these things the man has with him when he comes into the other life and he is successively brought into a full recollection of them. This is his Book of Life, which is opened in the other life, and according to which he is judged. People can scarcely believe this, but yet it is most true.

Arcana Coelestia 2474

The Final Barrier

But to be unwilling to die on account of one's children is natural both with the good and the evil; for the evil also love their children, but for the sake of the ends which prevail in themselves, namely, that they may shine with honours, and so forth.

Spiritual Diary 1236

Time and Space

Angels do not know what time is although with them there is a successive progression of all things, as there is in the world, and this so completely that there is no difference whatever and the reason is that in heaven instead of years and days there are changes of state.

Heaven and Hell 163

Spaces in heaven are simply the external conditions corresponding to the internal states.

Heaven and Hell 193

Any one in the spiritual world who intensely desires the presence of another comes into his presence, . . . and conversely, one is separated from another so far as he is averse to him.

Heaven and Hell 194

All things in heaven appear, just as in the world, to be in place and space, and yet the angels have no notion or idea of place and space.

Heaven and Hell 191

The Real World

It was shown me . . . what the ideas of children [in heaven] are when they see objects of any kind. Each and every object seemed to them to be alive.

Heaven and Hell 338

All the angels have their own dwellings in the places where they are, and they are magnificent. I have been there, and have sometimes seen and marvelled at them, and have there spoken with the angels. They are so distinct and clearly seen that nothing can be more so. In comparison with these, the habitations on earth amount to scarcely anything. They also call those which are on the earth dead, and not real; but their own, living and true, because from the Lord. The architecture is such that the art itself is derived from it, with a variety that knows no limit. They have said that if all the palaces in the whole world should be given them, they would not receive them in exchange for their own. What is made of stone, clay, and wood is to them dead; but what is from the Lord, and from life itself and light itself, is living; and this is the more the case that they enjoy them with all fullness of the sense.

Arcana Coelestia 1628

These gardens are presented with such life before the external sight that those who are there not only see them, but perceive every particular much more vividly than the sight of the eye perceives such things on earth . . . . Each and all things there appear in their most beautiful spring-time and flower, with a magnificence and variety that are amazing; and they are living, each and all, because they are representatives.

Arcana Coelestia 1622

In the other life colors are presented to view which from their brightness and resplendence immeasurably surpass the beauty of the colors seen on earth; and each color represents something celestial and spiritual.

Arcana Coelestia 1053

A certain person who had been much talked of and celebrated the learned world for his skill in the science of botany, after death heard in the other life, to his great surprise, that there also flowers and trees are presented to view; and as botany had been the delight of his life he was fired with a desire to see whether such was the case, and was therefore carried up into the paradisal regions, where he saw most beautiful plantations of trees and most charming flower gardens of immense extent. . . . He was allowed to wander over the field, and not only to see the plants in detail, but also to gather them and bring them close to his eye, and to examine whether the case was really so. [2] Speaking with me from thence he said that he could never have believed it. . . . He said further that he saw an immense abundance of flowers there which are never seen in the world, . . . and that they all glow with an inconceivable brightness because they are from the light of heaven. That the glow was from a spiritual origin, he was not yet able to perceive, that is, that they glowed because there was in each one of them something of the intelligence and wisdom which are of truth and good. He went on to say that men on earth would never believe this, because few believe there is any heaven and hell, and they who believe only know that in heaven there is joy, and few among them believe that there are such things as eye has not seen, and ear has not heard, and the mind has never conceived.

Arcana Coelestia 4529

Telepathy

The speech of an angel or spirit with man is heard by him as audibly as the speech of man with man, yet by himself only, and not by others who stand near; and for the reason that the speech of an angel or spirit flows first into a man's thought, and by an inner way into his organ of hearing, and thus moves it from within; while the speech of man with man flows first into the air and by an outward way into his organ of hearing, and moves it from without. Evidently, then, the speech of an angel or spirit with man is heard within him; but as the organs of hearing are thus equally moved, the speech is equally audible.

Heaven and Hell 284

By means of his natural mind, raised to the light of heaven, man can think, yea, speak with angels; but the thought and speech of the angels then flow into the natural thought and speech of the man, and not conversely; so that angels speak with man in a natural language, which is the man's mother tongue.

Divine Love and Wisdom 257:2

In heaven every one speaks from his thought, since speech there is the immediate product of the thought, or the thought speaking.

Heaven and Hell 2

In the entire heaven all have the same language, and they all understand one another, to whatever society, near or remote, they belong. Language there is not learned but is instinctive with every one, for it flows from their very affection and thought.

Heaven and Hell 236

Thought brings presence.

Divine Providence 29; 50:2; 326:2

Any one in the spiritual world who intensely desires the presence of another comes into his presence, for he thereby sees him in thought, and puts himself in his state.

Heaven and Hell 194

Angels

All the societies in the heavens are distinct in accordance with their uses [to others]. . . .Some societies are employed in taking care of little children; others in teaching and training them as they grow up; others in teaching and training in like manner the boys and girls that have acquired a good disposition from their education in the world, and in consequence have come into heaven. There are other societies that teach the simple good from the Christian world, and lead them into the way to heaven; there are others that in like manner teach and lead people from the various non-Christian nations. There are some societies that defend from infestations by evil spirits the newly arrived spirits that have just come from the world; . . . and there are some that attend upon those who are being raised from the dead.

Heaven and Hell 391

When newcomers into the spiritual world are in this first state, angels come to them for the sake of wishing them an auspicious arrival, and at the first they are greatly delighted from conversations
with them.

Five Memorable Relations 6

Heaven is a kingdom of uses. There is no one there who does not
discharge a use. The kinds of uses are innumerable, . . for there
are, there, those who instruct others, those who lead to good,
those who are with men, those who awake the dead, those who
protect, and those who are responsible for others.

Spiritual Diary 5158

The celestial angels who are with the one that is resuscitated do
not withdraw from him, because they love every one; but when
the spirit comes into such a state that he can no longer be affili-
ated with celestial angels, he longs to get away from them. When
this takes place angels from the Lord's spiritual kingdom come,
through whom is given the use of light; for before this he saw
nothing, but merely thought. . . . the angels are extremely careful
that only such ideas as savor of love shall proceed from the one resuscitated. They now tell him that he is a spirit. When he has
come into the enjoyment of light, the spiritual angels render to the
new spirit every service he can possibly desire in that state; and
teach him about the things of the other life so far as he can comprehend them. . . . The angels do not withdraw from him, but he
separates himself from them; for the angels love every one, and
desire nothing so much as to render service, to teach, and to lead
into heaven; this constitutes their highest delight.

Heaven and Hell 450

Suggested Reading

General

Atwater, P. M. H. *Beyond the Light: What Isn't Being Said about Near-Death Experience*. New York: Carol Publishing Group, 1994.

———. *Coming Back to Life: The After Effects of the Near-Death Experience*. New York: Ballantine Books, 1991.

Bailey, L. W., and Jenny Yates, eds. *The Near-Death Experience Reader*. New York: Routledge, 1996.

Brinkley, Dannion, with Paul Perry. *At Peace in the Light*. New York: HarperCollins, 1995.

———. *Saved by the Light*. New York: HarperCollins, 1994.

Eadie, Betty J., with Curtis Taylor. *Embraced by the Light*. Placerville, California: Gold Leaf Press, 1995.

Gallup, George, Jr. *Adventures in Immortality*. New York: Mc-Graw-Hill, 1982.

Giles, Chauncey. *The Nature of Spirit and of Man as a Spiritual Being*. Charleston, South Carolina: Arcana Books, rpt. 1997.

Harris, Barbara Whitfield. *Spiritual Awakenings: Insights of the Near-Death Experience and Other Doorways to our Soul*. Deerfield Beach, Florida: Health Communications, Inc., 1995.

Harris, Barbara, and Lionel C. Bascom. *Full Circle: The Near-Death Experience and Beyond*. New York: Pocket Books, 1993.

Kastenbaum, Robert. *Between Life and Death*. New York: Springer, 1979.

Kirven, Robert. *Angels in Action: What Swedenborg Saw and Heard*. West Chester, Pennsylvania: Swedenborg Foundation, 1994.

Lundhal, Craig R. "Angels in Near-Death Experiences," *Journal of Near-Death Studies* 11, no. 1 (Fall 1992): 49–56.

_____. *A Collection of Near-Death Readings*. Chicago: Nelson Hall, 1982.

Mitchell, Janet Lee. *Out-of-Body Experiences*. New York: Ballantine Books, 1981.

Moody, Raymond, Jr. *Life after Life*. Atlanta: Mockingbird Books, 1975.

_____. *The Light Beyond*. New York: Bantam, 1988.

Morse, Melvin, with Paul Perry. *Closer to the Light: Learning from the Near-Death Experiences of Children*. New York: Villard Books, 1990.

_____. *Parting Visions: Uses and Meanings of the Pre-Death, Psychic, and Spiritual Experiences*. New York: Villard Books, 1994.

_____. *Transformed by the Light: The Powerful Effect of Near-Death Experiences on People's Lives*. New York: Villard Books, 1992.

Rhodes, Leon S. "The NDE Enlarged by Swedenborg's Vision," *Anabiosis* 2 (June 1982): 15-35.

_____. "Reports on Eternal Life," in *Emanuel Swedenborg: A Continuing Vision*. Ed. Robin Larson et al, 237–240. New York: Swedenborg Foundation, 1988.

Ring, Kenneth. *Heading toward Omega*. New York: William Morrow, 1984.

_____. "The Impact of Near-Death Experiences on Persons Who Have Not Had Them," *Journal of Near Death Studies* 13, no. 4 (Summer 1995): 223–235.

_____. *Life at Death: In Search of the Meaning of the Near-Death Experience*. New York: Coward, McCann and Geoghegan, 1980.

_____. *The Omega Project: Near-Death Experiences, UFO encounters, and Mind at Large*. New York: William Morrow, 1992.

Sabom, Michael. *Recollections of Death: A Medical Investigation*. New York: Harper & Row, 1982.

Warren, Samuel M. *A Compendium of the Theological Writings of Emanuel Swedenborg.* 1875. Reprint, New York: Swedenborg Foundation, 1979.

Woofenden, Lee. "Death and Rebirth." Unpublished M.A. thesis, Swedenborg School of Religion, Newton, Massachusets, 1995.

Writings by Emanuel Swedenborg Related to Near-Death Experiences

Arcana Coelestia. Trans. J. F. Potts. 12 vols. 1905–1910. Reprint, West Chester, Pennsylvania: The Swedenborg Foundation, 1995–1997.

Divine Providence. Trans. John Ager. 1899. Reprint, West Chester, Pennsylvania: The Swedenborg Foundation, 1996.

Heaven and Hell. Trans. John Ager. 1900. Reprint, West Chester, Pennsylvania: The Swedenborg Foundation, 1996.

———. Trans. George F. Dole. New York: The Swedenborg Foundation, 1979.

The Spiritual Diary. Trans. G. Bush, J. Smithson, and J. Buss. 5 vols. 1883–1902. Reprint, New York: Swedenborg Foundation, 1978.

Additional Resources

The International Association for Near-Death Studies (IANDS) is the only organization dedicated exclusively to the study of the near-death phenomenon. It provides public information about NDEs, sponsors scholarly research, and serves as a clearinghouse and support network for experiencers. IANDS publishes the quarterly *Journal of Near-Death Studies* and also issues *Vital Signs*, a quarterly newsletter. For more information, contact: IANDS, P.O. Box 502, East Windsor Hill, Connecticut 06028; tel: (860) 528-5144.

Conversations with Angels:
What Swedenborg Heard in Heaven
Edited by Leonard Fox and Donald Rose
Newly translated and arranged by theme,
remarkable conversations with angels;
selected from Swedenborg's writings.
*Swedenborg's conversations with angels
startle the reader with insights into the reality of the spiritual world . . . . , an engaging,
fascinating contribution to angelic studies.*
—*Reviewer's Bookwatch*
0-87785-177-8

A Psychology of Spiritual Healing
Eugene Taylor
Draws from psychology, the world's religions, and spiritual experience to show
how true healing comes from within.
*. . . Taylor's creative vision, impeccable schol-
arship, and daunting range of interests . . .
will dramatically impact the psychology of
health and consciousness.*
—*Jeanne Achterberg*
0-87785-375-4

A Thoughtful Soul:
Reflections from Swedenborg
Edited and translated by George Dole
Foreword by Huston Smith
Newly translated selections from
Swedenborg . . . hold a door ajar for those
unfamiliar with this scientist-turned-
metaphysician.—NAPRA ReView
*[Swedenborg's] theology is about as practical
as one could ask. Asceticism is not the way to
God. . . . A good person is saved with any reli-
gion or with no religion. —Gnosis Magazine*
0-87785-148-4

Light in My Darkness
Helen Keller
Edited by Ray Silverman
Foreword by Norman Vincent Peale
Keller's 1927 spiritual autobiography
revised; Keller states that "Swedenborg's
message has been my strongest incitement
to overcome limitations."
*Presents an inspiring picture of this remark-
able woman's affirmation of the power and
triumph of the spirit. —New Age Retailer*
0-87785-146-8

Emanuel Swedenborg:
A Continuing Vision
Edited by Robin Larsen
A pictorial biography and anthology of
essays by such contributors as Jorge Luis
Borges and Czeslaw Milosz.
*The richest book for the dollar we have seen
in 14 years of reviewing books for Brain/
Mind Bulletin. —Marilyn Ferguson, author
of Aquarian Conspiracy*
0-87785-136-0 HC, 0-87785-137-9 PB

 **To order these and other
Chrysalis titles, or works of
Emanuel Swedenborg:**

Individuals: call (800) 355-3222
to place an order or request a free catalog or
write: Swedenborg Foundation Publishers •
PO Box 549 West Chester, PA 19381

Booksellers: call (800) 729-6423
or write to place an order: SCB Distributors •
15608 S. New Century Drive • Gardena, CA
90248